FORT CASEY

THE HISTORY OF FORT CASEY
AND THE DEFENSE OF THE PACIFIC NORTHWEST

by Terry Buchanan

PUBLISHED BY SERENITY RIDGE PRESS

Published by
Serenity Ridge Press

Copyright ©2010 Terry Buchanan. All rights reserved. No part of this publication may be reproduced in any format without the permission of the publisher.

For all inquiries, please email: info@serenityridgepress.com
www.serenityridgepress.com

ISBN 978-1-4276-4628-6

Printed in the United States of America

First Edition

This book is set in Weiss.

Designed by Magdalena Bassett, BassettStudio.com
Photo scanning and restoration by DJ Bassett, HistoricPhotoPreservation.com

This book is dedicated to those men who served at Fort Casey and all the Coastal Defense installations in the Pacific Northwest. Because there were no great battles or military actions in the Puget Sound, theirs is a story that has gone somewhat unnoticed. For over 45 years the men of the Coast Artillery manned Fort Casey in good times and bad but they were always there, ready to defend our nation. To the thousands of men who passed through and served at Admiralty head this book is dedicated.

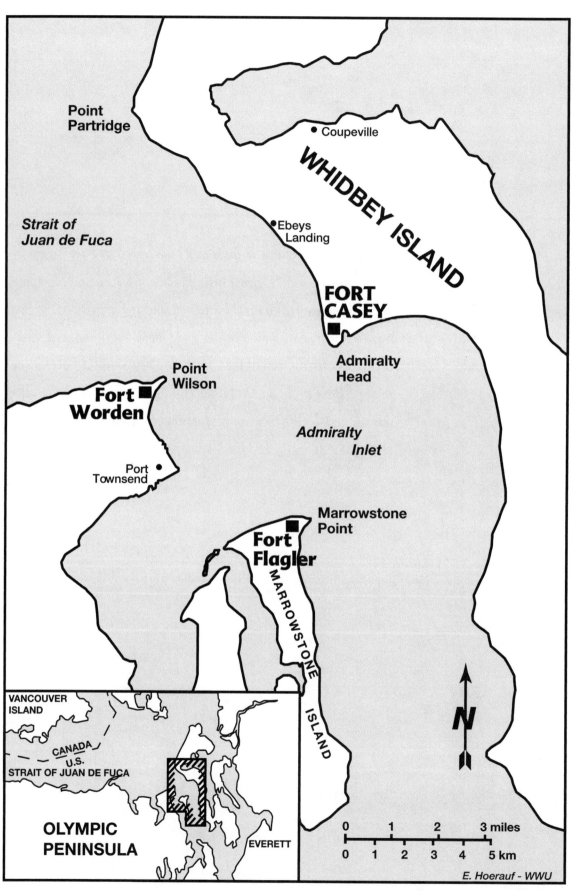

CONTENTS

CHAPTER 1
Coastal Defense in the Puget Sound .... page 7

CHAPTER 2
Construction: 1897 - 1910 .... page 27

CHAPTER 3
The Golden Age: 1900 - 1918 .... page 45

CHAPTER 4
World War I at Fort Casey .... page 65

CHAPTER 5
1918 - 1937: The Decline Begins .... page 77

CHAPTER 6
World War II .... page 93

CHAPTER 7
1945 to the Present .... page 121

EPILOGUE .... page 142

APPENDIX A
Fort Casey Gun Battery Histories .... page 147

APPENDIX B
Fort Casey's Main Armament .... page 153

CHAPTER FOOTNOTES .... page 166

INDEX .... page 187

FORT CROCKETT BLOCK HOUSE, built in 1848 near the present day Fort Casey reservation. These types of structures served as a potential refuge for local settlers and their families in the event of trouble with native tribes.

CHAPTER ONE

Coastal Defense in the Puget Sound

Guarding the entrance into the heart of the Puget Sound waterway are a number of empty and abandoned coast artillery fortifications. Like silent sentinels, these concrete gun emplacements were positioned to defend the only deep water navigable approaches to Seattle, Tacoma, Bremerton, and other points in the great natural expanse that is Puget Sound. They were a key part of a defense system designed to prevent a hostile fleet from reaching the Bremerton Navy Yard and the heart of the Pacific Northwest. One of these coast artillery emplacements is Fort Casey.

Fort Casey was built on a bold point of land on the westward side of Whidbey Island called Admiralty Head. The fort was located on one of three naturally formed, strategically valuable extensions of land within the main entrance to the Puget Sound. The guns of the fort projected out toward the deep waters of Admiralty Inlet, near the place where the Inlet branches southward from the main Juan de Fuca Strait.

Across the inlet to the southwest lies Point Wilson, near the city of Port Townsend. On the bluffs and beach overlooking the waterway Fort Worden was constructed. Further to the south from Point Wilson lies the third natural defense position into the waters of the inlet, Marrowstone Point. On the bluffs of the point Fort Flagler was erected. The forts built on these three land extensions formed a natural triangle that became the cornerstone of the Puget Sound Coastal Defense.

Established during the late 1890's, Fort Casey, along with her sister forts Flagler and Worden, is an example of the first extensive project undertaken by the United States for the protection of the important section of the Pacific Northwest lying north of the Columbia River. Taken in a much broader sense, Fort Casey is a prime example of a type of defense installation used at one time in the military program of the United States. It is symbolic of a great strategic idea which once dominated American military planning and for a time gave the United States a system of harbor defenses unexcelled by those of any other nation.[1]

The giant rifles of Fort Casey and the other forts of Admiralty Inlet were never called upon to fire their guns in defense nor were they ever associated with any outstanding events in history. In spite of this, the forts of Puget Sound occupy a prominent place in the history of the Northwest. Designed to be an essential part of the overall defense of the nation, for a brief period of time, Fort Casey and the other forts of Admiralty Inlet were the guardians of the gate. They were the sentinels that were meant to provide fifty years of armed insurance. As coast artillery installations they reflected theories that directed our national defenses in the years before the advent of the modern battleship and the airplane. These forts also present a point from which the broad story of coastal defense, most particularly at Fort Casey, can be told.

Coastal Defense is a topic that can be traced back over two hundred years in our nation's history. The protection of seacoast cities and merchant trade from marauding ships was of great concern long before the American Revolution and continued as late as World War II. The reasons for this concern for seacoast fortifications stemmed from a combination of geographical, historical, and traditional considerations. Thus seacoast fortification became more than just an attractive means of defense. The emphasis on this particular form of protection continued to grow until it was virtually an obsession and led, toward the end of the nineteenth-century, to a program of harbor defense that superceded any other form of military policy.[2]

Through the first century of this nation's history the greatest potential threats of invasion came not from other neighboring countries in this hemisphere, but from across the seas. In addition, the unique geographic character of the coastline, with its numerous harbors and coastal cities, simply had more exposed points than did most other nations. During the Revolutionary War, the value of Coastal Defense was clearly demonstrated. On June 28, 1776, a British fleet with 50 ships and an army of 3,000 men, attempted to enter Charleston Harbor, South Carolina. They were met by deadly fire from a seemingly impregnable fort constructed of Palmetto logs and dirt. After a ten-hour duel the British withdrew and left Charleston alone for the next four years.[3]

Experiences in the War of 1812 similarly proved the point. Shore batteries had the decided advantage over ships. Only under the most favorable conditions, such as overwhelmingly superior firepower or overall naval superiority that losses could be afforded to capture a strategic position, would ships oppose coastal forts. A maritime power of Britain's magnitude was capable of going against the odds but not so for the fledgling U. S. Navy. From that time onward to the middle of World War II, when air power finally became dominant over gun power, American military doctrine dictated that defenses would be provided for all important seaports, coastal cities, and naval bases.[4]

These were not, however, the only reasons for the preoccupation with coastal defense in the United States. There were a number of other traditions that had endured from colonial times to shape the national defense policies. One was that of the citizen soldier and a dislike for a large standing Army. The practice of preparing in peacetime for the eventuality of war fit the concept of coast defense nicely. Strong fortifications could be prepared in times of peace and left relatively idle and unmanned until needed. When the security of the nation was threatened, the civilian soldier would be called to fill the military need and the means of defense would be the forts. This would prove time and again to be totally inadequate to provide for the defense of the nation but the belief persisted in the minds of those who commanded the most control, the political leaders who appropriated the money.

Closely related to the militia tradition was the American tendency toward fortifications and armaments of an economical nature. Defensive emplacements did not require large numbers of men for operation and even less to maintain. Again seacoast fortifications ideally fit this concept. Lieutenant Henry W. Halleck wrote:

> *When once constructed they require but little expenditure for their support. In time of peace they withdraw no valuable citizens from the useful occupations of life. Of themselves they can never exert an influence dangerous to public liberty; but as the means of preserving peace, and as obstacles to an invader, their influence and power are immense.*[5]

His use of the phrase "... as the means of preserving peace," reflects upon another tradition common in the United States - that with the right military hardware war could somehow be avoided. Much like the weapons systems of the present, the coast defense was the technical achievement of its day that would provide the nation with security. It was non-aggressive in appearance and yet would preserve the peace by its presence alone. The fortifications were an assurance that we would stay out of any foreign wars, an idea that was particularly strong in the years leading up to World War I. This belief became so reassuring that in the War Department reports and the military publications of the 1890's interest in the Coastal Defenses of the country became almost obsessive.[6]

President Grover Cleveland, in his annual message of December 6, 1896, summed up this combination of traditions out of which our seacoast fortifications emerged, by emphasizing the security it provided. He pointed out that though it was essentially passive in nature, it still provided a sense of security: "*... it is neither the purpose nor the effect of such permanent fortifications to involve us in foreign complications, but rather to guarantee us against them.*"[7]

A majority of the American public and a succession of Congresses that were naïve to true militarily realities firmly believed in these traditions and continued to approve huge expenditures of money for the construction of coast defenses. The view that the construction of permanent seacoast fortifications was a way to keep the nation out of foreign entanglements worked to reinforce one of the nation's most deep-seated traditions regarding war. Each new expenditure was thus justified through a faithful adherence to the notion that such construction offered the hope of avoiding war altogether.[8] Whether these fortifications did in fact succeed is always open for debate. Our participation in two world wars seems to denigrate the value of weapons of deterrence and yet out defenses in the Continental United States were seldom challenged even when they had long become obsolete.

The need for defense in the Pacific Northwest grew slowly as the region gradually increased in population and importance. Although for many years there was little to protect as settlement was irregular and the local Indians were generally peaceful, the potential strategic importance of the Puget Sound was noted by various explorers and military leaders. Captain George Vancouver of the British Royal Navy was the first to truly explore the waters of Admiralty Inlet and the Puget Sound. During his famous voyage to the Northwest Coast in 1792, Vancouver and his men explored and named many of the area's most notable landmarks including Admiralty Inlet, Whidbey island, and of course Puget Sound.

During the months that were spent exploring, Whidbey Island was circumnavigated by a group of Vancouver's men and landings were made at the site of the future Fort Casey. Other landings were made at Point Wilson where Fort Worden would one day be located. The obvious potential military value of these land extensions at the entrance to Puget Sound did not escape the well-trained British officer.

American explorers also visited the region and were aware of its value. One of the first formal mentions of the potential military value of the area came from a Frenchman serving in the United States Army. Benjamin Louis Eulalie de Bonneville, after serving as a geographical explorer and fur trader in the Northwest and later as commander of Fort Vancouver, Washington, mentioned in his report dated March 26, 1837:

> *I beg leave to call your attention to the topography of 'Pugitt's Sound' and urge in the most earnest manner that this point should never be abandoned. If the United States claim, as I hope they ever will, at least as far as 49 degrees of north latitude, running due west from Lake of the Woods on the above parallel we shall take in 'Pugit's Sound.' In a military point of view, it is of the highest importance to the United States.*[9]

At the time of Bonneville's report, however, there was very little that needed protection.

The argument of 'What is there to protect?' would be used for many years in defining areas in the Pacific Northwest for defense. There seemed to be more urgent needs elsewhere in the growing

American nation. With the settlement of the Oregon controversy in 1846 and the Mexican War in 1848, the United States began to take steps to provide for the protection of the immense new territory it had acquired. A joint commission of Navy and Corps of Engineers Officers was empowered by President Polk on November 30, 1848. These officers were instructed by the War and Navy Departments to examine the entire Pacific Coast, between San Diego and Puget Sound, and select those points most suitable for the construction of coastal fortifications. The Commission was accorded this immense task and yet little in the way of funding was provided to properly carry it out. The vastness and irregular nature of the coast presented numerous problems in the areas of communication, logistics, strategy, and tactics. Sites selected for fortification had to be able to resist direct attack and deal with potential threats within their prescribed defense sectors. With these requirements in mind the Commission looked principally at defensible anchorages or harbors as the primary means of defense. These bases would be fortified and could serve as places of refuge for vessels endangered by an enemy's cruisers.

The Commission issued its report on November 1, 1850, and recommended only three defensive sites for immediate construction: San Francisco, San Diego, and the mouth of the Columbia River. Suggested fortifications at the entrance to Puget Sound, including one on the western side of Admiralty Inlet, were relegated to a "third class" priority, those to be built "at a remote period."[10] There were a number of other potential defense sites selected in the Northwest, some of which were given a higher priority for fortification by the commission than Admiralty Inlet but they too were designated for construction at a future date. The lack of settlements in the area, the distance across the waterway entrance (which at that time was greater than artillery of that period could effectively protect) and the huge projected cost undoubtedly affected the decision concerning Admiralty Inlet. Reports of the Commissions findings also show that defensible harbors, even though they might be in remote locations, were considered, at that time, of more importance than a commanding bluff.

This somewhat dim view concerning the defenses north of the Columbia was not shared by all. Officers on the Pacific Coast and high officials in the War Department felt a need was there and not of a "third class" nature. Officers stationed in the area and those traveling through came away impressed with the sheltered harbors of the Sound and the need for some type of defensive fortifications. General Persifor F. Smith, commanding the Army's Division of the Pacific Northwest at Steilacoom, was very impressed with the need for effective protection in the Puget Sound Region. In his report to the War Department, dated October 7, 1849, he referred to the superior harbors of the Sound. He recommended that strong defensive fortifications would be needed to protect the entrance to Admiralty Inlet. In the list of batteries he recommended for immediate construction along the Pacific Coast was one at the entrance to Admiralty Inlet.[11]

In the following years the matter of coastal defense on the Pacific Coast was passed from one board to another. Little money was appropriated for surveys and it was left to the local area commanders to do their own inspections and to send in periodic reports. One such survey of note was carried out in May of 1855 when, by order of the Commanding General of the Pacific Department, Captain George Stoneman, Second Cavalry, and First Lieut. W.H.C. Whiting, Corps of Engineers, was dispatched to inspect possible fortification sites in the Puget Sound area.

Upon their return they reported at length on the Indian tribes in the area and specifically of the potential dangers of attack by the Northern tribes living in British and Russian territories. They pointed out the need for establishing military garrisons that could adequately respond to these dangers at such locations as Bellingham Bay and Point Defiance. They also recommended that they be reinforced by small, swift steamers, armed with howitzers for protection.[12] In addition, their survey dealt with the subject of the region's defense with regard to foreign powers. The board voiced a concern that would be expressed by other military leaders in years to come, that of acquiring Vancouver Island. In their opinion the control of the Island by the English jeopardized the defense of the area and put the whole western coast in potential danger.[13] This report was forwarded to the Commanding General of the Pacific Department and, like many other reports, was simply filed away. The Military was slipping into a period of austerity and consequently very little was done to provide any kind of coastal protection except for the reservation of several tracts of public land for future military purposes. Years passed and nothing definite was done, a trend that would aptly describe coast defense in the Pacific Northwest for the next 40 plus years.

There were others, however, who added their voices to those of the Army officers on the coast calling for adequate defense measures. With the passage of the Donation Land Law in 1850, increasing numbers of homesteaders began staking their claims throughout the Oregon and Washington territories. Between 1851 and 1860 this new law brought a large increase in population to the coastal regions of Puget Sound in particular. Olympia, Steilacoom, Tacoma, Seattle, Port Orchard, Bremerton, Coupeville, Port Townsend, and Bellingham were just some of the communities founded in the coastal areas.

As the white settlements increased, the local Indians felt mounting pressure. They were being forced to give up their lands and their way of life. Government promises of payment for the land they had already relinquished and protection from further white infringement were never kept and trouble was inevitable even among the Puget Sound tribes, who were considered incapable of violence.[14] Although most of the real fighting took place in Oregon and Eastern Washington, there were acts of violence by both natives and whites in the Puget Sound. Cabins were burned, cattle driven off and travelers ambushed. Frightened settlers took refuge in hastily built block houses, converted churches, barns, or school houses. The local volunteer militia was hard pressed to catch or even control the marauding Indians. Efforts to provide protection and support for the local residents resulted in the establishment of Fort Bellingham and Fort Townsend during 1856 in addition to the already existing Fort Steilacoom, but all of these posts were little more than garrison stations and were practically useless for coastal defense purposes.[15] On February 19, 1857, the Oregon Territorial Legislature memorialized Congress for troops to be sent. This was but the first in a long series of petitions sent in the following years. This petition, like many others, received little response or was just ignored.

It was not until the late 1850's, when the San Juan Islands boundary dispute threatened hostilities between the United States and Great Britain, that there was some renewed interest in the defense of the area. Both military and local personnel sent pleas to Congress for some kind of protection. These pleas apparently spurred some interest because in December, 1858, Congress passed a resolution calling for the Secretary of War, John B. Floyd, to submit detailed plans for the proper defense of the Puget Sound. Secretary Floyd informed Congress on January 21, 1859, that there were no detailed plans and that none could be prepared until further surveys were carried out. He immediately made a request for a $10,000 appropriation to make the surveys but Congress refused. No funds were appropriated and the original request was tabled.[16]

In June of 1859, matters worsened in the San Juans when an American farmer, Lyman A. Cutler, killed a Hudson Bay Company pig that had wandered into his potato patch. That single shot was heard in Washington and London but apparently most clearly by Brigadier-General William S. Harney at Fort Vancouver. Misinformed about Cutler's treatment by the British, Harney ordered troops to proceed from Fort Bellingham to occupy the southern part of San Juan Island to protect American citizens and to oppose action by British officials.[17] The presence of American troops on the island caused the British Governor, Sir James Douglas, great concern as he believed the Americans might try to take control of the Island and claim sovereignty. Douglas had no troops at his disposal so he requested support in the form of British warships from Esquimalt on Vancouver Island. With British Naval vessels hovering off shore and the Americans constructing fortifications on the south end of the island, the situation over the death of one pig was quickly escalating a minor event into a major crisis. This event brought renewed calls for defense in the Puget Sound.

In July, Harney, as Commander of the Department of Oregon, made a personal visit to the military posts in the Puget Sound. In his official report that followed soon after his return, he took great pains to point out the lack of proper defenses in the area:

> *I would respectfully call the attention of our Government to the fact that we have neither a ship of war on Puget Sound or nearer than California, nor is there a gun in this department larger than a 6-pounder. With a sea-coast of greater extent than that of the Atlantic from Maine to Florida belonging to this command alone, our defenseless position all impose upon me the duty of urging a speedy action.*[18]

He ended his report by urging immediate action be taken in establishing permanent defensive fortifications at the mouth of the Columbia River and at various points of the Puget Sound.

The Corps of Engineers also found this an appropriate time to push a request of their own that was basically the same as Harney's. They presented Congress special reports calling for an appropriation of $100,000 to begin immediate construction of fortifications at the sites selected by General Harney. The Engineer's argument had no more effect than that of the General on loosening Congressional purse strings and no money was appropriated.

Attitudes in the nation's capital evidently changed as fears of an outbreak of hostilities between the United States and Great Britain in the Northwest grew. On November 9, 1859, the Secretary of War ordered the Chief of Engineers, General Joseph G. Totten, to make a personal inspection of the entire Pacific Coast, to select sites suitable for military and naval installations, and to indicate the character and extent of the fortifications required for proper defense.[19]

In his report, issued May 28, 1860, Totten, like many other officers, was greatly impressed by the strength of the British forces on Vancouver Island. He recognized that the naval base at Esquimalt commanded the Strait of Juan de Fuca and would dominate the small American squadron stationed on the Pacific Coast. He believed that should a war break out between the two nations, of necessity, the United States would be fighting a purely defensive action. In his report he stated:

> *The possession by a great naval power of the whole of Vancouver's Island.., at which, with naval mastery a command might be maintained at all times over the Straits of Fuca and all the waters within Cape Flattery, including, of course, Puget Sound and the San Juan Archipelago. This foreign possession, while it obscures somewhat the question of our defensive policy in that region, leaves it very clear that so long as that mastery is upheld all commerce of the inner waters through these narrow straits must, in time of war, be interrupted, or at least exposed to the greatest hazards.*[20]

General Totten acknowledged the superiority of foreign military forces in the region and therefore made endorsements that directly reflected a defensive posture. He placed a good deal of importance on the establishment of two heavily fortified harbors within the Straits of Juan de Fuca that could be used as places of refuge for both naval and commercial vessels in times of conflict. This concept was a direct reflection of the role many congressional and military leaders interpreted as the Navy's primary function. From the days of the Revolution, it was assumed that American naval power would always be in the form of commerce-raiding cruisers and merchant shipping. This popular conception had changed very little since 1776. The Navy's role was still directed toward maintaining a fleet for defensive purposes. Totten saw no major changes in the foreseeable future that would alter the military situation in the area and therefore structured his recommendations with this in mind.[21]

In his inspection of the harbors and settlements within the Puget Sound Totten found very little that he felt was worthy of protection. None of the harbors inside Cape Flattery, including Admiralty Inlet, had any establishment or populations that warranted protection by fortification; likewise, he could see no major changes in the near future. General Totten considered the area backwoods and apparently figured it was going to stay that way. He mentioned a number of growing cities in the region, including Seattle, Olympia, and Port Townsend, but perceived they were still very small. The report noted nothing inside of Cape Flattery worthy of importance even as in a second class of works.[22]

He conceded that the area collectively would be worth defending but that the price would be out of proportion to the value of any of the objects being protected. He stated that if it were possible to close the mouth of Admiralty Inlet with fortifications it would justify a large expenditure of money but that this was not possible. The distance across the entrance to the Inlet was too great for weapons of 1860 and he could foresee no improvements in ordnance that would make passage through the Inlet an enterprise of peril to an invading ship. He, therefore, recommended that the Puget Sound be guarded by a system of defenses further into the interior of the Sound, in the Foulweather Point vicinity.

General Totten finished his report by reemphasizing the importance of the harbors of refuge for American ships and for the urgency of action.

> *Though several times mentioned, I must here renew urgently the recommendation as to a Board of Engineers for this coast, and press its immediate organization and entrance upon the duty of making examinations, surveys, projects, and estimates. Everything has yet to be done here. Years must be consumed in the execution of any project or system, no matter what . . . I recommend with like earnestness the calling upon Congress to appropriate at the present session the sum of $100,000,000*

for commencing such fortifications as the President may find to be necessary for the defense of forts within Cape Flattery, Washington Territory. [23]

As respected as General Totten was, his recommendations brought little more response from Congress than any of those that had been presented earlier. The tension in the San Juans was easing and with the gathering storm of the Civil War approaching, little more was heard nationally about protecting the Puget Sound until after 1864. Local commanders continued to send out engineers to inspect possible fort sites and the War Department continued to ignore their recommendations.

In December of 1866, however, as part of an Executive Order setting aside land in the Northwest for military reservations, a new Board of Engineers for the Pacific Coast was established. Under the leadership of Major George H. Elliott, Corps of Engineers, this new board, like others before it, was directed to examine the waters of the Straits of Juan de Fuca and Admiralty Inlet and select sites for permanent and temporary fortifications as they deemed necessary. During their tour of the reservation sites, they visited Admiralty Inlet, Point Wilson, and Marrowstone Point. In their report, issued on December 9, 1867, they made a number of recommendations. One in particular would exert considerable influence upon Puget Sound defense plans for years to come.

The Board does not recommend the construction of any fortifications at the present time in the waters of Admiralty Inlet or Puget Sound, but it does advise that a Joint Board of Army and Navy officers be organized to select which of the harbors in these waters should be chosen as a naval and military depot, and when the selection is made that this harbor be fortified. [24]

The United States had for a number of years considered building a Navy yard in the Northwest. The presence of the British naval station at Esquimalt, with its excellent port and supply facilities and the lack of any such American convenience nearer than San Francisco, pointed up the need for such a military depot. The Board in its report was simply pointing out that the location of the Navy yard would be a big factor in the positioning of fortifications and favored waiting until the dry dock site was selected before making any recommendations for coastal defense positions. They also agreed with General Totten's view that any defensive construction would have to be located well within the Sound. They acknowledged the advances made in artillery power and range since 1860 but still believed the entrance to Admiralty Inlet was too wide to be effectively closed off by shore based forts.

Most of the recommendations made by the Board of Engineers for the Pacific Coast were in strong agreement with findings of Totten in his Report of 1860. This Board, and many that would follow, looked upon the work of the venerable Chief Engineer as an exhaustive study that was as complete as could be done. Their acknowledgements reinforced the recommendations made in Totten's report and these studies would continue to dominate military thinking concerning Puget Sound well into the 1880s.

The construction of harbor defenses in the United States slowed drastically in the years following the Civil War. In the years immediately after the war, construction activities were limited to renewed work on unfinished Third System forts. These were fortification projects built between 1816 and 1860 to provide at least some measure of added protection for the country. For the most part, however, these activities were not pursued with the enthusiasm that marked the pre-war years. With the Civil War over, Congress was in no mood to approve any further large amounts of money for military spending. On the contrary, postwar stresses led to reductions in all areas of military appropriations. In the twelve years after the War (Reconstruction period) the nation passed through fundamental changes altering the course of American history. The rise of industrial over agrarian priorities, the emergence of the Federal Government as a powerful, controlling force, and the resolution to the slavery question were of much more importance to the majority of people both in and out of public office. Reforming the nation after the tragedy of the war and disbanding the armies that had fought each other, took precedent over all else. There were also technical reasons for reconsidering coastal defense construction that were due to lessons learned in the war itself.

The Civil War's influence on the nature of arms produced some of the most momentous technical changes in the history of warfare, and these changes directly affected the entire United States system of coastal fortifications. Almost overnight and without exception the large, masonry forts of the pre-Civil War period, with their huge vertical walls and high density of heavy armament, were relegated to obsolescence.[25] The whole concept of vaulted chambers housing dozens of guns, usually set within the ramparts of a high walled, multi-leveled, stone structure was clearly shown to be no longer practical. The Civil War was also the proving ground for a revolution in ordnance, rifled artillery.

The invention of the cannon during the fourteenth century had lead to the end of vertical-walled fortification in land warfare. With the development of the cannon as a weapon of siege, it became obvious to military leaders and designers that masonry could never be expected to resist the fire of heavy, land based guns.[26] Nevertheless, seacoast fortifications continued to be built out of brick and stone. The reason why this practice continued for centuries had to do with the amount of fire power that could be accurately brought to bear at a particular section of a wall. Land based siege guns could be directed with sufficient accuracy against a small area of a wall to shatter it by repeated pounding. On the other hand smoothbore naval guns fired from moving vessels with unsteady decks lacked the accuracy and the numbers to concentrate enough fire at one particular point to breach masonry walls. Because harbor defenses continued to be built in the traditional way, they remained relatively impregnable.[27] The development of the rifled gun ended this invulnerability. Rifling, the cutting of spiral grooves on the inside of a gun barrel to make the projectile spin when it was fired, was not new when the Civil War started. It had been used in small arms as early as the 1500s and was found to be very effective in increasing range and accuracy. The application of rifling to heavy ordnance, however, was not accomplished with any real effectiveness until the 1850s. Even then, after rifled guns had proved their superiority, smoothbore artillery with its short range, questionable accuracy, and limited power continued to be the backbone of almost every army and navy.

In using smoothbore guns the weight and size of the projectile were fixed within unchanging limits. The size of the shot was limited to the diameter of the gun bore, and the weight was a physical constant based on the density of the metal.[28] Thus for many years guns were simply referred to by the weight of the shot they fired; "32-pounders" or "64-pounders". When the spherical shot was fired, it had nothing to stabilize it in flight. The round ball flew as it listed, and the direction of its flight was entirely dependent on how the shot left the gun's muzzle. What rifling did was to make it possible to gyroscopically stabilize the flight of a projectile. As a result it was now possible to develop an effective elongated shell which could be directed to fly point-first throughout its trajectory.[29]

The Civil War was to provide an unusually thorough testing ground for these new developments in ordnance. It also settled questions concerning masonry fortifications versus rifled artillery that had not been answered conclusively during the Crimean War of the previous decade.

The majority of Third System forts were completed when the Civil War broke out. Though a number of them had been in service for over thirty years, they were still some of the most spectacular harbor defense structures to come out of any era of military architecture. From the technical standpoint, this large group of massive, vertically-walled forts represented the fullest development of features which had previously appeared in only a few isolated instances, i.e., structural durability, a high concentration of armament, and enormous overall firepower.[30] Though most were only partially armed and largely unmanned, at the beginning of the war, the forts were structurally complete and it was not long before many of them came under fire. The performance of the Third System forts under artillery fire produced some revealing results. Fort Morgan, at Mobile, was engaged by a 100-pounder Parrot rifle at a range of over 3000 yards in July, 1864. One shot ricocheted from the crest of the covered way, struck the escarp wall and passed through, leaving a two foot hole. It still had sufficient energy to severely damage the casemates, where it eventually penetrated and lodged.[31] Fort Pulaski, in Georgia, was taken by Federal troops in 1862 after a long-range bombardment in which the southeast wall was successfully breeched with relative ease by batteries of both rifled artillery and smoothbores. Eye witness accounts speak of the rifled projectiles "boring into the brick face like augers" and the balls "striking like trip-hammers and breaking off great masses of masonry which had been cut loose by the rifles."[32] The fort surrendered in a day and a half.

In contrast, hastily-built fortifications of earth and sand, called provisional works, were surprising in their resistance. Both sides learned fairly early in the war the superiority of these earthwork defenses. Fort Wagner, hastily constructed with sand ramparts sixteen feet thick and with bomb-proof shelters protected by ample sand, held out for fifty-eight days under Federal bombardment. By taking shelter in the bomb-proofs during the artillery bombardments and then manning the parapets, the Southern defenders were able to beat off numerous attacks with just small arms fire. The effect of solid shot against the sand proved to be negligible. It was specifically noted that the shells thrown by rifled batteries were less effective. They mostly burst on striking and then threw up a mass of sand that fell back into the same place.[33]

With this experience in mind, the fortifications built after the fighting had begun were almost exclusively of the earth-work type. Both armies soon turned to the widespread use of sand bags and earthen emplacements. They were much simpler and quicker to construct, and far less costly than the brick and stone forts of the pre-war days. They were also much easier to repair, in some cases while fighting was in progress. Large numbers of these emplacements were erected during the war on inland rivers, around cities, and in several positions along the coast.

Military planners in Europe were seeking coastal protection in an altogether different way. In England the strengthening of the Navy and the long peace of 1815-1854 lead to a decline in fortifications. It was believed that the Royal Navy was unlikely to allow an enemy fleet to get close enough to do any real damage. With this belief in mind, harbor defenses were allowed to deteriorate into a run-down condition. Guns were allowed to rust, stores of powder spoiled from water seepage, parapets went un-repaired, and gun carriages were permitted to decay. Very little was done to maintain the coast defenses. The Crimean War, however, was the match which lit a slow-burning fuse and lead to a revival of interest both in England and the rest of Europe.[34]

The successes and failures of the Crimean War and the launching of the first iron-clad warship brought about a rethinking of defenses by European military leaders.[35] The wooden walls that navies had provided for their coastlines were now rendered obsolete overnight. The iron-clad warships also posed a real gunnery problem for land based defenses which could no longer count on enemy ships being forced to stay a considerable distance from shore when bombarding. The launching of the French iron-clad, the *La Glorie*, along with the resurgence of France under Napoleon III lead to a total re-examination of defenses against direct attack from the sea in England and other European nations.

In Britain the answer to iron-clad warships was a massive construction program built around strong armored enclosures or casemated batteries. These fortifications would be built of granite and brick up to fourteen feet thick, and each casemate opening would be covered with a wrought-iron armor shield that had a firing port for the gun. Most all of the forts were multi-leveled, with many feet of brickwork and concrete to give bomb-proof protection. England also embarked on an elaborate program of sea forts. These were masonry towers built on shoals or artificial islands in strategic locations, their purpose being to deny entry to an enemy where a large stretch of water could not be protected with shore batteries. Other European nations also were aware of the need for improved defenses and, like England, the main reliance was to be on stone and iron. France and Italy continued to build masonry-walled forts. While in Belgium they sought protection by turning Antwerp into a "National Redoubt".[36] Belgian engineer, Henri Brialmont, designed a ring of powerful fortresses around the capital city that were considered the most powerful in Europe. Though heavily reinforced with iron, these forts were still of brick and stone construction and proved to be vulnerable to rifled bombardment.

While these tremendously costly fortifications alterations were in progress in Europe, the American Civil War was drawing to a close. The reports that came from America on the comparative resisting power of masonry forts to rifled artillery caused some delays. The question of constructing earthworks fortifications over granite and iron was argued at length, particularly in England. There was, however, reluctance by some to put much credence into the reports from across the Atlantic. Many European nations considered the Civil War to be a barbaric conflict of little importance. The British took the results more seriously, but the question there was more one of economics. Their rebuilding program was just starting to show results; the cost of demolishing their granite and brick forts and starting all over with earthworks was out of the question. England's alternative was to move even more toward the use of iron.[37]

The use of iron sheathing was the beginning of a trend in military architecture which was to dominate European thinking and continue well into the twentieth century. American fortifications did not follow the European direction.[38] Military engineers could now see the vulnerability of existing seacoast fortifications and the value of less costly earthen emplacements. The United States, however, was in no position to commence building an entirely new system of harbor defenses no matter what the cost. Pre-occupation with domestic issues meant that little new construction was envisioned.

The planning engineers were also wary of new developments in ballistics. There was a real concern that an anticipated period of rapid advances in artillery might quickly make obsolete any new defensive work. This did in fact happen. Because of the reluctance to begin new construction for technical reasons, and more importantly, the lack of public or political support from a nation still war-weary, the possibilities of any large appropriations for coastal defense were out of the question.[39] Aside from minor work undertaken to complete certain Third System forts in the first two to three years immediately after the war, fortifications primarily designed and constructed in the mid-1800's defended the country. These old works, armed, for the most part, with smoothbore guns of Civil War or earlier vintage, remained the main components of the nation's harbor defenses.

While the defense of the coasts rested with smoothbore cannon and masonry forts of the Third System, the army was at work conducting experiments in ordnance and fortification construction. These experiments dealt with the possibilities of covering the external faces of existing masonry forts with iron plating and in the development of new and more powerful rifled guns. Like many nations in the world, the United States was trying desperately to keep up with the rapid advances being made in artillery and defense. Throughout the 1870's and 1880's records show constant competitions and trials carried out both in Europe and the United States.[40]

These tests pitted new designs in armor plating against constantly improving projectiles. Nations concerned with coastal defense were continually looking for the best weapons and the best protection. All these tests produced a wealth of information, most of which was only valid until the next trial took place. Each new development in armor was followed by new developments in projectiles capable of defeating it. The constant leapfrogging between armor and ordnance kept European engineers in a continual state of trying to catch up. In order to take advantage of each new development in armor protection or gun improvement, the modification of existing fortifications became a very expensive and protracted business. From 1860 to 1880, European nations struggled with advancing technology unable to stay up to date with their defenses. Many projects became outmoded before they could even be completed. The upgrading of existing works consumed huge amounts of money.[41]

In America, for the most part, these constant changes had to be ignored. New weapons of increased size and power were being developed and these guns were simply too large to be mounted in existing masonry forts. In the United States the majority of the sites in service were of this type. The weapons were also mounted on carriages that were more effective when they could be lowered below a parapet crest for loading and service. Used in this fashion even simple barbette batteries could be adequately protected. Thus, the inability of masonry to withstand modern weapons, the postwar shortage of funds for military purposes, and the need for emplacements large enough to receive the new armament combined in the closing years of the 1860's to bring about a return to an inexpensive mode of permanent fortification. Earth once again became the principal substance of protection.[42]

These new works, begun about 1870, were similar to the barbette batteries of earlier years. The emplacements were totally open, constructed of brick and concrete, but with magazines placed in more protected locations. The guns were now to be dispersed over a much wider area than the Third System forts with their massive concentration of weapons. For the first time these widely separated batteries functioned as the primary components of harbor defense rather than as a support role. Construction commenced on a large number of the new and comparatively inexpensive barbette batteries. Because of the simplicity of their construction, work proceeded rapidly, at least for a time. Unfortunately, the anticipated development of new weapons and their carriages did not progress as quickly, and existing smoothbore armament was installed in those works that reached completion. The new program also included other means of defense as well, such as large-caliber mortars, mines, and channel obstructions. The work on these defenses, however, never proceeded beyond the experimental stage. By 1875, Congressional appropriations stopped and this short lived coastal defense program came to a halt.[43]

Most of those works that had been started went unfinished and quite a few remained unarmed. Small annual appropriations continued for several years but this covered no more than nominal maintenance. With insufficient funds to provide adequate garrisons many of the completed and partially completed works were deserted and left to deteriorate. The simplicity of this new style of fortification quite probably was a factor that led to its rapid abandonment. Military leaders were apparently much more willing to surrender these modest brick and concrete parapets and rely on the much more elaborate Third System forts, obsolete though they were, for the defense of the nation.

While this new program failed to reach the desired goals it did mark a true turning point in American fortifications design. No longer would coastal defense forts depend upon single structures of stone and brick with their high concentration of armament. While the traditional storybook style forts of the early 1800s were still in use, never again would they be built in the United States.[44] The future of coastal defense now rested on dispersed individual batteries constructed in the most tactically favorable location that terrain would allow. Massive stone walls and casemated galleries were now abandoned in favor of widely separated guns of much greater size, protected, for the most part, by earth.

Aside from this short spurt of activity in the early 1870s, fortifications primarily designed and constructed in the mid-1800s and armed with smoothbore weapons of the Civil War were left to defend the country. Harbor defense construction was terminated, emplacements fell into disrepair, and during the late nineteenth century the defensive strength of the United States fell to perhaps its lowest point since 1812.[45]

While plans for the construction of the new, simpler style of fortification would not be implemented until the late 1890s, work continued throughout the 1870s and 1880s on the armaments intended for them. It was during this period of harbor defense inactivity that several critical advances took place in the design and production of heavy ordnance which would greatly affect America's future construction. These developments, which would revolutionize seacoast armament, involved the first large-scale use of steel for guns, the perfection of breech-loading, and the introduction of far more effective propellants.

The growth and maturing of the American steel industry enabled ordnance makers to use steel rather than iron in the manufacturing of heavy weapons.[46] By the late 1880's the combined availability of good quality steel in large amounts, industrial facilities for producing heavy forgings, and machining techniques meeting the required standards of precision, made it possible to produce a better weapon than ever before.[47] American ordnance was now able to produce great numbers of these lighter, stronger, longer, and much more powerful weapons.

Coupled with the development of these new, more powerful guns was the perfection of breech-loading. The loading of a gun from the rear, or through the breech, rather than through the muzzle, had been experimented with since well before the Civil War.[48] It would not be until the late nineteenth century, however, before steel manufacturing would reach a level of precision to produce the large, heavy, and extremely well machined blocks and recesses that successful breech-loading demanded.[49]

The perfection of breech-loading for heavy ordnance permitted the first really complete utilization of rifling. This in turn made possible the use of improved elongated projectiles that were far more efficient and effective. Breech-loading also allowed fortification designers to make better use of the new styles of gun emplacements that were developed. Carriages, the metal supports that held and moved the gun tube, were now designed to use the recoil of the weapon to lower it below the level of the parapets where it could be serviced with greater safety for the crew. All of these advances brought about an increase in the operating speed of the weapon and took the gun and its crew out of the view of the enemy.[50]

The third technical advance to ordnance was the development of new propellants for ammunition. Old-fashioned gunpowder had been used for centuries as an explosive charge but with the new, longer weapons being manufactured and the need for higher muzzle velocities it did not provide enough power.[51] With the use of these new developed ammunition propellants, gun tubes needed to be substantially longer than before and with the advances in steel manufacturing, already mentioned, this was now possible.

These technical achievements in heavy ordnance along with constant improvements in armor brought about changes of unheard of proportions throughout the world. They represented, within the space of a few decades, the greatest advances to be made in artillery between its invention in the fourteenth century and the appearance of the nuclear projectile in the mid-twentieth.[52] These changes affected not only the weapons being manufactured but the whole concept of defense. Countless millions of pounds, dollars, marks, francs, rubles and other currencies were spent on concrete and steel. Foreign nations felt compelled to spend enormous amounts of money trying to keep up with the changing technology and in most cases were unable to do so. From 1859 to 1890 England spent over 17 million pounds on various forms of coastal defense. The German fortifications at Heligoland, the Austrian fortresses in Poland, the Bucharest forts, the Italian and Spanish coast defenses, and the Russian works at Kronstadt in all probability cost sums far in excess of that amount.[53]

The revolution in ordnance also affected the defenses in America. In this country, however, this period of tremendous change and unrestrained spending occurring elsewhere in the world, from 1865 to 1890, had to be largely ignored. Some minor improvements to existing works were made and there was the short spurt of activity in 1870 but these were very small in comparison to construction in other nations such as England, Belgium, or Germany. While Europe struggled with the ironclad and the constant changes in weapons, American designers could only carry on with their experiments and plan for the future. In what can now be looked at as beneficial, the lack of funds for new fortifications spared the United States from building costly and what would soon prove to be vulnerable ironclad forts. It was much cheaper to pay for the endless surveys and recommendations from regional military leaders than to actually build the proposed fortifications. The nation was spared the expensive and protracted business of trying to keep up with the constantly changing technology that other nations were dealing with. American defenses eventually moved from the smoothbore weapons and masonry walled forts of the Civil War right into the breech loading, open emplacements of the 1890's without an intervening stage. The concepts and ideas for a new generation of defenses were present but money just was not available to implement them.

As the 1880s began, the coastal defense situation in the Pacific Northwest was much the same as it had been in 1860 when General Totten had completed his report. Year after year, the cries for construction of coastal defenses were ignored and nothing was done. Commanders of the Department of the Pacific, San Francisco, as well as those of the Department of the Columbia, Vancouver Barracks, besieged the War Department with pleas for the construction of coastal defense lines. Annual reports usually included references to the need for some form of fortifications at the entrance to Puget Sound. Old Fort Townsend was the only active military post left on Admiralty Inlet and was of no use at all for coastal defense. Brigadier General Nelson A. Miles repeatedly urged constructive action. The General argued:

> *The defense of the Pacific coast is of such national importance that I regard it neither wise nor patriotic to longer delay its improvement. We have not reached that perfection of human society in which it is safe to trust ourselves in a defenseless condition.*[54]

The government was still listening with a deaf ear. It was not just in the Pacific Northwest that money was lacking, harbor defense appropriations had been completely cut off since 1875 and coastal defense throughout the nation was left to deteriorate.

The reasons given for not building fortifications in the Northwest were basically the same ones General Totten had given some twenty years earlier. There still was really nothing of worthwhile importance within the Puget Sound which warranted an expenditure of the large sums of money needed to build fortifications. This, in point of fact, was very true. The Washington Territory had an estimated population of only 75,116 in 1880, of which 90 percent was rural. For the most part it was still an isolated frontier that had not begun to attract any large numbers of settlers. The Northern Pacific railroad would not be finished as a transcontinental connection until 1883 and the few cities within the Puget Sound that had any sizeable number of people were still decidedly frontier in nature. At least on this point Totten's report from 1860 was still true. The proposed location of a naval shipyard had, as yet, not been decided upon and it was still believed that Admiralty Inlet was too wide to be effectively closed off with artillery of that day. It appeared, at least, that the fear of a war with Great Britain had finally been put to rest as little was mentioned of the potential threat of the British on Vancouver Island.

Something of great importance that was changing during the early 1890s was the role of the Navy in national defense. The conservative philosophy of the Navy's role as one of commerce raiding and coastal protection was finally being challenged by American Military leaders. The most prominent and influential voice was that of Alfred Thayer Mahan. His writings helped to change the theories of continental protection into an instrument of genuine sea power. He believed that defending the coast and commerce raiding would seriously hinder the development of American naval strategy and naval technology. Mahan argued:

> *The Navy is not the proper instrument for coast defense in the narrow sense of the expression, which limits it to the defense of ports. The passive defense of our shores is properly the work of the Army. Furthermore if the defense of ports, many in number, be attributed to the Navy, the naval forces will be so divided that its real strength will be lost.*[55]

Mahan emphasized that the enemy had to be kept not just out of the ports but entirely away from the coasts. This could only be done with secure, protected bases from which to operate and by a strong, aggressive Navy. This called for the building of many new ships and the cutting of the umbilical cord between the Navy and coastal defense.[56]

If this new navy was not to be handicapped in defending harbors and seacoasts, the coastal defenses around the country would have to be improved. The old forts of brick and stone that had been built between the War of 1812 and the Civil War had proved obsolete and yet little had been done to improve them. Totten's concept of "Harbors of Refuge" was changing to "secured bases of naval power."

Concern over the condition into which the fortifications of the country had been allowed to deteriorate was finding more and more voices. In the Puget Sound this was just a continuation of the military pleas for construction of some kind. The Commanding General of the Department of the Columbia, Brigadier General Nelson A. Miles, finally wearied of the bureaucratic merry-go-round and acted on his own. In 1884 he appointed his own board of experienced officers and gave them orders to establish a plan of defense for the Puget Sound. This board surveyed the Sound and reached a conclusion that was a complete break with the Totten tradition. Their decision was a true reflection of the technological changes in ordnance that had taken place since the 1860's. These officers recommended that the principle reliance for the defense of Puget Sound should be placed upon batteries of 10-inch rifles and mortars "of the largest caliber and greatest penetration" upon Admiralty Head, Marrowstone Point, and Point Wilson. All three of these locations were at the entrance to Admiralty Inlet and not in the Totten concept to be considered harbors of refuge. The report went on to point out that all three sites were necessary and of equal importance, but they found that Admiralty Head, with about forty acres of cleared land, now under cultivation, "was the only position then in a condition for building of batteries and erection of the necessary buildings for a garrison."[57]

General Miles immediately gave his approval to the board's report and forwarded it to the War Department. In an effort to try to win approval and get some kind of congressional appropriation, General Miles sent along a personal plea and tried to point out that technical advances in artillery would now make it possible to defend Admiralty Inlet. General Miles pulled out all the stops to try to prevent a quick Washington rejection as he even attempted to resurrect the old fear of the British. He reminded Washington of the amount of money the British were spending on their navy yards at Esquimalt.

> *The British Government is now expending a very large amount of money in completing its navy-yard and dry-docks at Esquimalt, near Victoria, British Columbia, and has kept during the past ten years from a single ship-of-war to a small fleet in those waters, and I think it advisable that our Government should take an equal interest in the establishment of a naval station in this part of the United States.*[58]

In point of fact the Esquimalt Naval Station had been in operation since the late 1840s and for many years leading up to the dry dock being opened in 1887, there had been a desperate need for such a facility to service British ships. The only other one on the West Coast was at Mare Island, San Francisco, in the United States, which put the British at a disadvantage. Since Esquimalt had been designated as the Pacific Station headquarters for Her Majesty's Ships in 1862, the need for an improved repair facility was necessary. Both English and American governments had long fretted over the closeness of the British base to the Puget Sound but there is very little to indicate that there were ever any real ulterior motives by either nation. Local military leaders huffed and puffed over potential military conflicts and "what ifs" but during the only real threatening issues that ever came up - the Pig War of 1859 and the San Juan Islands dispute - both sides showed considerable restraint to take any real military action. By the 1870s the over all security of Britain's world-wide interests demanded forbearance and peaceful Anglo-American relations.[59]

All of the pleas from General Miles were, not surprisingly, to no avail, as the Chief of Engineers endorsed the report and then promptly shelved it, presumably with all the others, until the location of the naval depot could be settled. What did come of the efforts of the General was a fresh outlook toward Puget Sound. This was the first real break with the Totten concept and it made an impact on future events.

The growing concern for updating fortifications within the United States was finally heard, for in 1885, President Grover Cleveland, upon assuming office, appointed a special board to make a complete study of coastal defenses. The board, headed by the Secretary of War, William C. Endicott, was to review the entire coast defense situation and to submit recommendations for a program based upon the newly developing weapons. The joint Army-Navy-Civilian group that comprised the board found it had been assigned a task of monumental proportions. They conducted an extensive study of the whole subject of fortifications, the development of new armament, and the question of protective materials.

Early in 1886, the Endicott Board, as it became known, made its report to Congress. The program the Board presented was a dynamic, far reaching break with tradition that owed much of its recommendations to studies done in the years immediately after the Civil War. In examining the Board of Engineers studies they found much that they agreed with and felt was still practical in 1885. The Endicott Board called for the complete modernization of seacoast defenses in the United States. It recommended that multi-storied forts covered in armor with guns shooting through ports should be forgotten; that gun mountings capable of hiding the gun when it was not firing be used; that the heaviest calibers of guns available should always be used; that mortars or high-angle guns should be developed in order to attack warships through their decks, the most vulnerable spot; and that mines and obstacles should be placed in channels whenever possible. To implement these changes in technology they put forward a plan calling for the building of fortifications at 26 coastal locations and three on the Great Lakes. The plan also provided for floating batteries, torpedo boats, and submarine mines.[60] The cost of this program was estimated at $126,377,800.

The biggest changes brought about by the Endicott recommendations were in the physical nature of the fortifications themselves. The new gun emplacements would still be very costly but would be much simpler than before. Instead of the massive vertical-walled structures of the Third System, the new forts were built to blend into the surrounding landscape as much as possible. Another difference was the complexity of the weapons used. The heavy smoothbore cannons of the 1850s could be manufactured in a matter of days, but the new, rifled weapons took months of very painstaking, exacting work to produce. In addition to these changes there was the real diversity in the variety of weapons and how they would be used. The Board recommended three classes of armament. Besides the large guns of 8-, 10-, and 12-inch caliber, which were basically flat-trajectory weapons, there were also to be great numbers of high angled mortars. A third class of weapons, of five different calibers from 3-, to 6-inch, were designated as rapid-fire guns. These used ammunition light enough to be handled manually and had a rate of fire of five to fifteen rounds per minute. These weapons along with underwater mines and torpedo boats were to make up the new coast defense system of the country.

In terms of the estimated cost alone the proposal was grossly unrealistic. As might be expected the Congress just was not going to put out that kind of money and in fact waited four years before voting any funds at all. Moreover, the type and quantity of new weapons called for by the program were not as yet developed. It was not until 1890 that Congress finally voted $1,200,000 in appropriations. This would be followed up with further annual sums. In the time interval between the Board's report and the releasing of money the new breed of ordnance was perfected and because of the unexpectedly high performance these weapons achieved, the planners were able to reduce the number of guns needed.

As construction began in the early 1890s the Board's recommendations were further reduced with some thirteen hundred guns and mortars of 8-inch caliber and larger pared down to less than seven hundred actually installed. The harbors of Boston, New York, and San Francisco were given priority for construction, the remaining recommended sites for building to be implemented when money was available.[61] What this did was to classify the 29 fortifications sites recommended by the Board into a priority list. Those positions that were deemed most important would get funding when it became available first and other sites further down the list would have to wait. This was obviously not what the Board had in mind with its recommendations but the unrealistic size of its proposal and the unwillingness of Congress to appropriate larger sums of money slowed things considerably.

Although Puget Sound was among the waterways surveyed by the Board, it was not regarded as worthy of consideration for fortification and was not on the prioritized list of 29 sites. This omission raised a mild howl of protest in the Senate and an even bigger one from military leaders in the area. The response was to cite the time-worn excuse concerning the location of the navy yard as the main reason. Responses to these protests at least made it evident that Totten's plan was finally laid to rest. The technical developments in ordnance and the changing attitude toward the Navy's role no longer made the "Harbors of Refuge" concept necessary. In 1888, the official reports concerning fortifications on Puget Sound made by the Chief of Engineers pointed out that it was now practicable to set up a first line of defense at the entrance to Admiralty Inlet.[62]

Military leaders continued to make pleas to the War Department on the need for fortifications in the Puget Sound and in particular the difficulties that had arisen with residents living on the government reservations. At three of these sites, New Dungeness, Point Wilson, and Admiralty Head, settlers were occupying most of the land. It was reported to the Adjutant-General of the Army on December 27, 1887:

> *During my visit to some of these reservations a few days ago I discovered them occupied by the dwellings and farms of citizens. An investigation disclosed the fact that in some instances parties held patents from the Government 'at the time' the reservations were set aside; in others that the settlers occupied the ground at that time, and perfected their titles and had patents issued to them afterwards, and in still other cases, patents were issued 'by the Government' for portions of these so-called reservations long after the reservations were declared.* [63]

Through the inaction of the Federal Government much of the reserved land was now owned as private property and would have to be purchased back from the local residents.

Continuing pleas from the military, a rapid growth of population in the Puget Sound, and more concern from the Federal Government concerning defenses in the Northwest finally achieved some direct action. On March 27, 1888, the Senate passed a resolution calling for the Secretary of War to prepare a report relative to fortifications in the Puget Sound. Secretary of War Endicott ordered all letters and documents from the Chief of Engineers and the Adjutant Generals Office that pertained to the need for defensive works upon Puget Sound. The materials were gathered and on April 27, 1888, Secretary Endicott turned over these documents to the Senate as House Executive Document No. 165. In this document Secretary of War Endicott fully endorsed a personal letter from the Chief of Engineers, Brigadier General J. C. Duane, as to the need for defensive fortifications of some kind in the Puget Sound. Duane also pointed out the need for urgency in the selection of the site for the proposed naval station.[64] The seventy plus page report was accepted but, not surprisingly, little was done.

The last barrier preventing construction of fortifications within the Puget Sound was finally removed in 1891 when the Congress selected Port Orchard as the site for a dry dock facility. The need for a large naval shipyard and dry dock had been voiced as early as 1867 but it would be until March of 1891 before an amendment to the Naval Appropriations Bill authorizing money for its construction, secured by Washington Senator John B. Allen, would finally pass Congress. The dry dock was completed by 1896 and almost immediately engineers began recommending fortifications for the defense of the Navy Yard.[65]

It was now left to a local board of officers and engineers, known as the Fortification Board, to choose the sites for the projected construction. Despite the fact that the location of the Navy Yard was known by 1891 and the continuous dialogue of reports flowing to the War Department, it was not until 1894 that a decision was made. The Fortifications Board selected eleven sites in the Puget Sound which were suitable for construction. One of the sites selected was Admiralty Head on Whidbey Island.

In following the recommendations of the Endicott and Fortification Board reports, Army engineers estimated that the following armament would be required for defense at the Admiralty Head installation: Batteries of 10-inch rifles mounted on disappearing carriages and 12-inch mortars. Additional armament added in later years would be 6-inch rifles mounted on disappearing carriages, 5-inch rapid-fire rifles on balanced pillar mounts, and 3-inch rapid-fire guns on pedestal mounts. Underwater mines or torpedoes, as they were called in 1900, were never used in the entrance to Admiralty Inlet. Because of the deepness of the Inlet and the swiftness of the current it was considered impractical. Anti-torpedo nets were used in the dock area of Port Townsend on occasions and mines were planted elsewhere in the Sound. The arrangement of the forts designated four lines of defense. The first line would consist of emplacements at Point Wilson, Marrowstone Point, and Admiralty Head. A smaller installation to block Deception Pass would be located to the north. The other lines would be located deeper within the Sound. Actual construction was still a number of years away but Congressional activity, sluggish as it was, began to take effect. The cattle leisurely grazing in the pastures owned by Dr. John Kellogg would soon find their grassland scarred by construction. Admiralty Head was soon to become part of the nation's coastal defense system.

CHAPTER TWO

CONSTRUCTION: 1897 - 1910

In March of 1837, one of the first recorded observations was made pertaining to the military value of fortifying the entrance to "Pugitt's Sound." Captain Benjamin Bonneville, a Frenchmen serving in the U. S. Army, made this recommendation recognizing the obvious defensive potential of the land extensions into Admiralty Inlet, something that was evident to all who sailed into the swift waters from the Straits of Juan de Fuca. Some 60 years later the Federal Government determined it was time to take action concerning this military potential in the name of national defense.

In June of 1896, Congress authorized funds for construction of gun emplacements at three locations on Admiralty Inlet: on Point Wilson, Marrowstone Point, and Admiralty Head. Within two months of this authorization, Army engineers appeared at Admiralty Head, making surveys and preparing the site for construction. No ground was actually broken, however, until April of 1897.

When the tracts of land in Puget Sound were reserved for the military in 1866, the order had had no effect on Admiralty Head. Most of the available land in the area already had been covered by donation claims.[1] The land around Admiralty Head had already been sold prior to the government's receiving of land for military use. Except for a tract of ten acres, the site of the government-owned lighthouse on the tip of the point, the land was owned by local residents. Military leaders mistakenly had assumed that the 640 acres set aside at Admiralty Head by the Executive Order of September 22, 1866 was theirs. This small question of ownership did not stop the Army Corps of Engineers, though, who commenced surveys while the matter was being settled. On April 20, 1897, a section of land encompassing 123 acres was purchased from Dr. John C. Kellogg, for the price of $7,200.00 dollars. This tract formed the basic reservation for the military post.[2] In the next few years, as the fort grew, additional land was purchased from residents around this initial site. By 1945 the total area of the land owned in fee by the United States within the boundaries of the fort reservation was 525.45 acres.[3] The total estimated cost of purchasing this land, which the military should already have owned, was $40,418.05 dollars.[4]

The Corps of Engineers complained that the failure to obtain the original site "as early as desired" had "seriously delayed the progress of construction work."[5] Weather, faulty construction materials, and mechanical difficulties of all sorts would prove to be much more time consuming than convincing the local farmers to part with their favorite pastures. An even greater issue would be the labor force. As the War Department was awarding its bids for work at Admiralty Inlet, gold rush fever was peaking in the Pacific Northwest.

During the summer of 1887 gold was discovered in Alaska and almost 100,000 men, mostly from the United States, were flooding across the International Border into British Territory. Just about every employer in the northwest found their work force deserting their daily routine to venture north and strike it rich. The private contractors hired by the Corps of Engineers to build what would soon become Fort Casey were to struggle with this problem of an unstable work force throughout the entire building process. The reasons for this labor shortage were not just the Klondike Fever but also the poor wages being paid, and the isolated location. The workers that could be found were less than highly motivated and unwilling to travel into the wilds of Whidbey Island to work on some dull government project.

When a sufficient workforce was finally contracted, the design of Fort Casey was similar to other coastal defense fortifications constructed in Puget Sound. All the forts followed a basic

ABOVE: The first lighthouse at Admiralty Head, built in 1860. It was moved to make room for the construction of the main gun emplacements. The building was later disassembled by a retiring Casey soldier and rebuilt near the town of Langley, on Whidbey Island.

RIGHT: The primary weapon installed would be the disappearing rifle. Built in caliber sizes from 6-inch up to 14-inch, these state of the art weapons would provide protection for the gun crews and massive fire power for defense. This rifle is in the up or firing position.

LEFT: This disappearing rifle is in the down or loading position.

BELOW: Construction on the main gun emplacements which would become Batteries Worth and Moore. Note the worker sitting on the framing and the scrapping teams in the distance. The construction required the removal of 40,000 cubic yards of earth by mule pulled scrapers and a work crew of about 80 men.

blueprint developed by the Corps of Engineers in response to the findings of the Endicott Board. Variations usually came about because of ground conditions and locations. The Corps was in charge of supervising the construction, but most of the work was sub-contracted out to private firms. An assistant engineer representing the Corps of Engineers was assigned to Casey throughout the years of its construction.

The initial contract for excavation and erection of four 10-inch gun emplacements was awarded to the Everett firm of Maney, Goerig & Rydstrom, a company with little reputation and less experience in projects of this potential size. The contract was approved by the Chief of Engineers on August 13, 1897, and the price agreed upon for the construction of these first works was $84,980.50. The contract called for the moving of some 40,000 cubic yards of earth on the bluff back of the lighthouse. To perform this work, a crew of about eighty men, recruited from up and down the Sound, was hired at $1.65 a day. This rate of pay, apparently, would have satisfied the men until they learned that in taking the job they also had to board at the Contractor's cook house at a weekly cost of $4.50 for meals. When the workers found out about this, they decided to go on strike. The Company tried to find a replacement crew but were unable to do so anywhere in the area. They were forced to settle the dispute by increasing the men's pay to 25¢ an hour or $2.00 for an 8 hour day.[6] Strangely, after this settlement was reached, very few of the men were actually paid the agreed upon wage. A weekly labor report sent in to Corps of Engineers Headquarters by the Corps Assistant Engineer, Philip G. Eastwick, list less than half of the men hired as receiving the 25¢ an hour pay. Most worked for 20¢ or less. The total weekly cost for the work done during the last week of January, 1898, after the strike settlement, came to $381.65.[7] The $2.00 a day would be the basic pay scale for men working at Admiralty Head well into the first decade of the 1900s.

To add to the delays in construction, the first shipment of Belgian cement brought in was rejected by inspectors. Government policy dictated that all materials for the forts were to be purchased in or from American manufacturers except in cases when it was in the best interest of the U.S. to make purchases abroad. This was what the Corps of Engineers was forced to do with cement. At the time of building, there were no quality cement producing plants in the area; for the emplacements on Admiralty Head, and virtually all the other works in the Sound, cement was imported from Belgium. The cement was brought in by boat in 400 pound barrels, with the first shipment of some 3,500 arriving in November of 1897. Government testing performed on samples for fineness (passing the contents of a barrel of cement through a No. 100 sieve) and for hardness (mixing concrete - allowing it to dry for 25 days and then testing it for the weight required to break it) proved unsatisfactory and it was rejected. New cement did not begin arriving until February of 1898.

A third delay to construction was the weather. With actual work not beginning at Admiralty Head till October of 1897, rain and winter storms hit the construction sites very hard. A storm on November 17, in particular, did great damage to the wharf, the pile driver tied to the wharf, and in general turned the work sites into seas of mud. It would be the early part of 1898 before real progress would occur. The construction began with the building of an Engineer's wharf, to be used almost exclusively by the Corps of Engineers, and the excavation of the emplacement site. The original lighthouse, built in 1860, was moved back from the bluff so that horse and mule powered teams of scrapers could begin moving earth. A mess hall and bunk house were erected down from the emplacement site along Crockett's

Lake. A number of temporary buildings were erected among these - an Engineer's office building, a water tank, and a cement-mixing shed. A well was also sunk for water. The grading and installation of a trolley line from the wharf crossing the beach was also begun. This would be used to bring materials from the Engineer's Wharf to the construction site. By the later part of 1898 a 3-foot gauge railroad line would be installed from the beach area. This line would be extended to each emplacement site, as needed, to bring work equipment, concrete, and heavier materials, such as gun tubes and carriages, to the finished works.

On November 16, 1897, the Chief of Engineers approved plans for a battery of sixteen 12-inch mortars on Admiralty Head. This had been part of the original recommendation for weapons at the fort. This new contract was awarded to the same firm already working at Admiralty Head, Maney, Goerig & Rydstrom. Work on the mortar emplacements began late in January of 1998.

An event of consequence effecting Admiralty Head occurred on February 15th, 1898: the Battleship *Maine* blew up in Havana Harbor, with a loss of two hundred sixty officers and enlisted men. Though there was no evidence to prove Spain was responsible, the jingo American press held them guilty and raised the cry, "Remember the *Maine!*" Before the official Navy report of the *Maine* explosion was completed, Congress unanimously voted a national defense appropriation of $50,000,000 million dollars. This boost in appropriations speeded up progress in the coastal defense program. With the outbreak of war with Spain and the threat of a Spanish bombardment, as unlikely as that was in the Pacific Northwest, work on the emplacements was rushed. In addition, at Admiralty Head, the weather was finally cooperating, good cement arrived, and the contractors had learned how to operate the concrete-mixing plant and move large amounts of concrete up to the work sites. Once these things got somewhat coordinated, work at the sites moved rapidly.

In February of 1898 labor problems again arose, as a sub-contractor working on the mortar excavations suddenly left. In his monthly work report Assistant Engineer Eastwick, wrote concerning earthworks:

> *The graders worked only on the lst and 2nd of the month. After the subcontractor, Mesers. o'Kelly & Sheehan, withdrew and went to Everett ostensibly for the purpose of reorganizing his force and returning. He has not since appeared and though promising the contractors that he will resume work it appears probable that he has abandoned the work.*[8]

A new sub-contractor from the local area was soon hired and within a month work resumed at the site.

Throughout the rest of 1898, work at Admiralty Head and the other forts of the Sound proceeded at a steady pace. There were still mechanical problems with the cement mixing plant, a temperamental railroad engine, shortages of gravel, and delays in receiving construction materials, but overall progress definitely was being made. The railroad line was extended from the main emplacements to the mortar site and huge quantities of concrete were poured. By November carriages for both mortars and the disappearing guns had arrived and a good deal of finishing work was in progress.

All three of the Admiralty Inlet forts benefited from the increase in military activity caused by the Spanish-American War. It had evidently not been intended, in 1896, to make the forts as large

ABOVE: Construction on a mortar pit at Fort Worden which gives a good example of how work progressed on the batteries at Fort Casey. The holes are for the concrete pads that will hold the mortars. The mule powered scrapers can be seen working at the back of the pit.

RIGHT: A completed mortar pit at Casey with the weapons installed. The landscaping of the hillsides has not been completed yet which would cause considerable problems when the guns were test fired.

ABOVE: Concrete work has been completed on the emplacements for 4 – 10" disappearing rifles by the Corps of Engineers. Only the gun carriages have been installed. Note the wood framing at the bottom. The Corps was having a difficult time stabilizing the bank and would eventually add a third 10" battery, Kingsbury, to the main emplacement.

BELOW: A 10" gun tube being brought up to the parapet for mounting. A small tram engine brought the barrels from the dock and would push the 35 ton tube up to the emplacement for mounting on its carriage. Note the bucket line from the dock area bringing rock to the cement shed for mixing to be poured at Kingsbury.

as they were now fast becoming. The plan apparently had been to maintain an "efficient garrison" at centrally located Marrowstone Point, from which troops could be sent to the other two forts as occasion demanded. Quarters at these latter points were to be limited to those necessary to house the small detachments required to guard and maintain the batteries.[9] It became very evident after the start of the War that these plans had changed. It now appeared that the Army intended to develop Fort Casey into a much more formidably armed installation and that it would be manned by a large, permanent garrison. Whether this was all due to the Spanish-American War is hard to determine.

Ever since the construction of the forts began there had been a good deal of political jockeying by different cities along the Sound. Each was trying to get a major military post built in their area. What resulted, by some accounts, was a mountain of red tape and construction proceeding at a snail's pace.[10] It is doubtful that this was the case. Work at Fort Casey, as has already been mentioned, was delayed by a combination of events, some dealing with nature and some with labor and materials, over which local politicians had no real control. It can be taken for granted that construction at just about any military installation will move faster in times of war than during peace but to surmise that political bickering and local jealousies caused the many delays in the work at Admiralty Head is an embellishment of the actual facts. To say that political leaders in say Tacoma, who favored having fortifications built closer to their municipality, caused construction delays at Admiralty Head is not only reading too much between the lines but is perhaps adding words. In any event with the war and the additional appropriations, the three posts were all steadily enlarged.[11]

On July 13, 1899, plans were received at Admiralty Head for the construction of emplacements for two 5-inch rapid fire guns. Work would begin by the end of the month. During 1899, work was essentially completed on the 10-inch emplacements and on the 12-inch mortars. Dressing the surrounding landscapes of both sites would continue well into the next year, as would mounting the carriages and gun tubes. The guns and their mountings were brought to the Engineer's Wharf by scow and then were loaded onto a railroad flat car that would slowly bring them to the emplacements. Ramps had to be built from the railroad tracks up to the gun level of the terreplein. Tracks were laid up the ramp and the small gauge engine would gingerly push the flat car with the huge barrels and carriage parts up onto the concrete platform of the emplacement. All the work of assembling the sophisticated carriages and placing the enormously heavy gun barrels onto the carriages was done by hand. Ropes, pulleys, mules and man power did what cranes and diesel engines did some 68 years later when 10-inch guns were once again brought to Admiralty Head. The new reservation at Admiralty Head had received its official name by the end of 1899. By General Order No. 134, Headquarters of the Army, Adjutant Generals Office, the post was named "Fort Casey" in honor of Brigadier General Thomas Lincoln Casey, last Chief of Engineers, United States Army.[12] Casey was remembered in newspaper publicity of the time as one of the "best-known and best-loved" officers of the War Department.

The first troops to arrive in the area for the purpose of taking official control and manning these close-to-completed forts in Admiralty Inlet arrived at Fort Flagler on Marrowstone Island, September 5, 1899. Fort Flagler, at this time, was the headquarters for Coastal Defense in the Sound; thus, all incoming Coast Artillery troops would report there to await assignment. Soon after their arrival, a garrison of thirty men, from Battery B of the 3rd Artillery, under the command of Lieutenant Alfred B. Putnam, was sent by boat to Fort Casey. These men lived in tents behind the main emplacements while cantonment barracks and other quarters were being built. Their first assigned duties were to help in the installation of the guns and provide guards for the post. The mounting of the main weapons was completed by January, 1900. On February 7th, 1900, Lieutenant Putnam had the honor of taking command of all ordnance and stores at Admiralty Head from the Corps of Engineers, and this officially activated Fort Casey as a military post.[13]

Work at the new 5-inch gun emplacement went slowly during the remainder of 1900. A serious accident occurred in May when the locomotive derailed while pulling a load of concrete to the building site. The engine climbed a split rail and went off the tracks overturning the concrete car. There were minor injuries to the engineer. Delays in the arrival of materials again slowed progress and in fact construction was stopped totally for a number of months late in the year due to a lack of funds. It seemed the contractor was running into large cost overruns and was passing it on to the Federal Government. Monthly appropriations were having trouble keeping up with the rising costs.[14]

The work being done at the 10-inch disappearing rifles and mortar emplacements was mostly concerned with the installation of more specialized equipment and the readying of the batteries for actual use. With the close proximity of salt water and the fact that the majority of the fortifications at each emplacement were underground, waterproofing and weatherizing everything became an ongoing task. The store rooms and magazines below the guns were constantly being treated for leaks and dampness. The magazines, in particular, where powder and shells were to be stored, were specially equipped. Each room had a thermometer to monitor temperature and was lined with copper sheeting and cedar. Unfortunately, in the case of some of the magazines at the main emplacements, leaky walls became a fact of life that was never corrected. Heavy blast-proof iron doors were hung at all doorways with some as large as 10-feet wide. Shot and shell hoists were installed to bring ammunition from the underground rooms up to the gun platforms for loading. All of this was protected by reinforced concrete walls, up to 12-feet thick in some places.[15]

In November, 1900, word was received of plans for a new 10-inch battery. This two gun emplacement would be connected to the existing 10-inch works and would just about bring Casey's main armament up to the standards recommended in 1894. Work would begin almost immediately.[16] By the end of the month, the time had finally come for the test firing of the completed 10-inch rifles and the mortars. One can only imagine the anticipation and excitement that must have been present as the first giant 10-inch disappearing rifle was raised to its firing position or the squat, ugly mortar was pointed skyward. One can only imagine the effect the sound of these monsters' firing must have had on the milk production of the nearby farmer's dairy herds. On November 30th and December 1st each of the four completed 10-inch rifles was test fired with full service charge. Aside from some minor cracks in concrete and a few broken lights everything went as it should have. At the mortar pits one gun from each of the four emplacements was test fired, lobbing its 700 pound projectile over the surrounding hillside and out into the Sound. As with the 10-inch rifles, there was no appreciable damage to the walls or earth slopes. However, the reports made to the Corps of Engineers Headquarters concerning the test firing does mention that the wooden doors to the latrines in each of the pits were damaged. The concussion from firing the huge caliber gun literally exploded the wooden doors off their hinges. This happened in all four pits. In a footnote at the bottom of the report a recommendation was made to install iron doors in place of the wooden ones as soon as possible.[17]

ABOVE: The tram was used to bring the gun tubes up from the dock and then to push it up the ramp to the parapets for mounting. The ramps were built and the tram tracks were laid up to the emplacement

BELOW: Construction begins on the three main barracks facing the parade grounds.

ABOVE: The main barracks under construction.

BELOW: The completed main barracks each capable of housing 109 soldiers. They had their own kitchens, cooking staff and dining rooms.

From early 1901 onward work at Fort Casey steadily increased. In April, excavation for the new 10-inch guns was underway and a guard house was built. By the end of May, a graded road had been built behind the mortars and the railroad tracks had been laid to the new 10-inch emplacements. The July report stated a new cement mixing plant had been built, the wharf had undergone major repairs, the bunk house and mess hall had been enlarged, a post warehouse had been constructed and word was received that the new emplacement would have three guns instead of two. Also completed during July were plans and specifications for a new Admiralty Head Light Station. They were completed by the 13th Light House District Office in Portland, Oregon, but construction would not begin until well into 1902, due to delays in selecting the most suitable site.[18]

With the fort growing as fast as it was, the need to acquire more land for the reservation arose. As early as March of 1900, recommendations were being made by local military boards to expand the post boundaries to the north. This was done in 1901 through condemnation. The local farmers again were told that national security demanded that they sell more of their land. Purchased through the condemnation process were 227 acres of land to the north of the original reservation running along the inlet.[19] In early 1902 the post officially took control of this new track of land. Two farm houses, into which the Post Ordnance Sergeant and the Post Surgeon promptly moved, and some smaller buildings were also acquired.

With this addition, Fort Casey almost doubled in size and plans were now made for future construction. On February 20, 1902, the Commanding General of the Department of the Columbia appointed a board to fix the location of the buildings of the enlarged post made possible by this additional land. The recommendations of this board constituted the basic plan of Fort Casey during the remainder of its existence as a military post.[20] The board laid out a parade ground occupying most of the low, level land at the neck of Admiralty Head. Along the south edge of this parade ground a row of barracks, with auxiliary structures was planned. Quarters for the post commander and other officers were projected low on the slope at the north end of the neck. The wharf built during the first construction period was to be rebuilt and enlarged.

The construction of these new buildings was turned over to the Quartermaster Corps of the Army, while the Engineers continued with work on the fortifications and their support facilities. Work was begun early in the year on both Battery Command Stations and the Fire Commander's Headquarters. Each gun battery would eventually have its own battery command station from which the firing of the guns was directed. The post Commander's headquarters, from which all activity connected with the operation of the fort was handled, would be a three level structure located very near the new lighthouse.

As work on these new buildings began, the first regular garrison force arrived. Composed of six officers and some 200 enlisted men of the 63rd and 71st companies of Coast Artillery, they arrived at Casey on June 28, 1902. The troops had been brought up from Alcatraz Island in San Francisco Bay, to Seattle and, finally, to the Puget Sound Artillery District Headquarters at Fort Flagler. They were then ferried over to Casey and quartered in the temporary barracks on the hill overlooking the planned parade ground.

As each new building and emplacement reached completion they were officially turned over to the Coast Artillery and the responsibilities of the Engineers or Quartermaster Corps ended. Most of the time the soldiers stationed at the fort began using the structures before they formally had been turned over but the Army followed its jurisdictional rules. In most cases, the C. A. did not accept a building or emplacement until it had been finished to the satisfaction of the inspector. Once possession had been officially taken by the Coast Artillery, the Army was responsible for maintenance.

Work progressed quite rapidly during the next few years. The construction of buildings and gun emplacements was enlarging fortifications at Admiralty Head to substantial proportions. The parade ground was cleared of stumps and leveled, and the new lighthouse was brought into service. The work on the Engineer's wharf was completed in August of 1903 and by the middle of the next year the majority of the new buildings had been finished. Work was completed on the main enlisted men's barracks. These were large two storied structures with stone foundations, frame walls, balconied porches and slate roofs. When finished, they provided living quarters for 109 men and each was equipped with its own kitchen and dining hall. Also turned over to the Artillery were Commanding Officer's quarters, quarters for officers and non-commissioned officers, a coal shed, and a quartermaster and commissary storehouse.[21]

This was not the end of the building construction. Records show that one or more new structures were completed during nearly every year between 1904 and 1910. An additional officer's quarters was added in 1905; a fire station, hospital rooms, blacksmith shop, quartermaster workshop, and a non-commissioned officer's quarters were completed in 1906; a gymnasium with a bowling alley was erected in 1908; an additional non-commissioned officers' duplex and various storage structures were finished in 1909. The last major accomplishment of the building program prior to World War I was the construction of a central power house in 1910. Built of reinforced concrete, it was located near the dock area below and to the south of the mortars, and would at last provide electricity on a permanent basis to the fort.[22]

At the same time this building boom was in progress, the armament of Fort Casey was increased. A concern had been voiced on a number of occasions, by military experts who regularly inspected the fort, that there was a real lack of smaller caliber support fire. It was believed that the main batteries of 10-inch rifles and 12-inch mortars were sufficient for long range bombardment but that protection was needed against close-in ground assault. To supplement the post's main emplacements, small caliber gun batteries were needed to provide this additional protection, a further deterrent, should large numbers of ships attempt entry into the Sound. In response to these concerns, four new batteries of guns were added to Fort Casey's armament between 1903 and 1908.

By the end of 1903, work was well under way on a battery of four 6-inch disappearing rifles. They were to be located along the bluff to the south of the main emplacements. Because of delays in the delivery of construction materials, a problem with the stability of the ground on which the emplacement was being built and the fact that the guns themselves did not arrive until 1908, this battery was slow to be completed. Another battery of two 6-inch disappearing guns was completed by 1905. It was located on the coastal bluff north of the parade ground. Like the other 6-inch battery, delays prevented it from coming into service until 1907.

Two smaller batteries of 3-inch rapid-fire guns also were added during this period. The first was located on the eastern side of Admiralty Head near its tip. The guns were connected to the 6-inch emplacements and overlooked the wharf area. The second 3-inch battery was installed on the low

ABOVE: The new Admiralty Head lighthouse under construction in 1902. It was a much more elaborate lighthouse that the first structure, with a circular brick tower, about 25 feet high, and a two-story brick keeper's house. A number of support buildings were also constructed at the same time including a mule barn behind the lighthouse.

bluff fronting Admiralty Inlet near the southwest corner of the parade ground. Both batteries were completed during 1905 but not officially turned over to the Coast Artillery for service until 1907.

The last of the 10-inch batteries to be built originally was to have been a two-gun set connected to the already completed four 10-inch rifles. By 1901, the battery was increased to a three gun emplacement, as a third gun would now be built in a position to allow it to fire at the inner sections of Admiralty Inlet. It was determined that none of the heavy rifle armament at any of the three harbor forts had this capability. This would be the only heavy gun that could shoot at an enemy vessel after it had sailed past the forts. Planners felt that they should be prepared for every possible military eventuality. Work was completed in 1904, but not turned over until 1905. It was officially accepted on November 27th, but as a two-gun battery. It was decided to make one of the already completed 10-inch emplacements a three gun set. They did this by incorporating one of the new 10-inch guns and its facilities into the existing battery. The new work therefore, was accepted as a two gun emplacement.

In December of 1904, the ten gun emplacements at Fort Casey were given names. This followed an Army tradition of naming batteries of guns in honor of fallen war heroes. These were not the men of which history books would give lavish accounts, but soldiers who had served their country in far flung battlefields, many in foreign lands. General Order No. 194 officially designated each of the batteries to be named as follows:

Battery Henry Kingsbury Two 10-inch rifles
Named in honor of Colonel Henry W. Kingsbury, llth Connecticut Volunteers who died September 18, 1862, of wounds received in action at Antietam, Maryland, September 17, 1862 during the Civil War.

Battery James Moore Three 10-inch rifles
Named in honor of Brigadier General James Moore, Continental Army, who served with distinction during the Revolutionary War, and who died April 9, 1777.

Battery William Worth Two 10-inch rifles
Named in honor of Brigadier General William Scott Worth, for his meritorious service at Petersburg and Appomattox during the Civil War and in the attack on San Juan Hill July 1, 1898 during the Spanish-American War.

Battery John Valleau Four 6-inch rifles
In honor of 1st Lieutenant John Valleau, 13th U. S. Infantry, who was killed in assault on Queenston Heights, Upper Canada, October 13, 1812 during the War of 1812.

Battery Thomas Parker	Two 6-inch rifles In honor of Brevet 1st Lieutenant Thomas D. Parker, U. S. Army (2d lieutenant, 2d U. S. Infantry), killed in action at Gaines Mill, Virginia, June 27, 1862 during the Civil War.
Battery Reuben Turman	Two 5-inch rapid fire rifles Named in honor of 2d Lieutenant Reuben S. Turman, 6th U. S. Infantry, who died July 2, 1898, of wounds received in action at San Juan Hill, Cuba, July 1, 1898 during the Spanish-American War.
Battery John Trevor	Two 3-inch rapid fire rifles Named in honor of 1st Lieutenant John Trevor, 5th U. S. Calvary, who died September 29, 1864, of wounds received in action at Winchester, Virginia, September 19, 1864 during the Civil War.
Battery Issac Van Horne	Two 3-inch rapid fire rifles Named in honor of Captain Issac Van Horne, Jr., 19th U. S. Infantry, who was killed in action at Fort Mackinac, Michigan, August 4, 1814 during the War of 1812.
Battery Schenck	Eight 12-inch mortars Named in honor of Lieutenant Colonel Alexander Dubois Schenck, for meritorious service in the battles of Bull Run, Stone River, Perryville, and Hoover's Gap during the Civil War.
Battery Seymour	Eight 12-inch mortars Named in honor of Major Truman Seymour, 6th U. S. Artillery, for meritorious service in the battles of Cerro Gordo, Centraras, and Cherubusco. He also took part in the Florida hostilities against the Seminoles, 1856-1858. At the outbreak of the Civil War he commanded his battery in defense of Fort Sumter.[23]

Construction during the first decade of the 20th century had proceeded at a rapid pace. Despite continual labor shortages, faulty machinery, delays in the delivery of all types of materials from cement to the actual weapons, and contractors who might best be described as in over their head, Fort Casey somehow was completed. Dr. Kellogg probably would not have recognized his cow pasture could he have seen it in 1910. What had been projected as a small outpost had become part of the nation's coastal defense. New construction would continue at Fort Casey but never at the pace or in the quantity that took place from 1897 to 1910. Admiralty Head now bristled with weapons to protect and defend Puget Sound and America.[24]

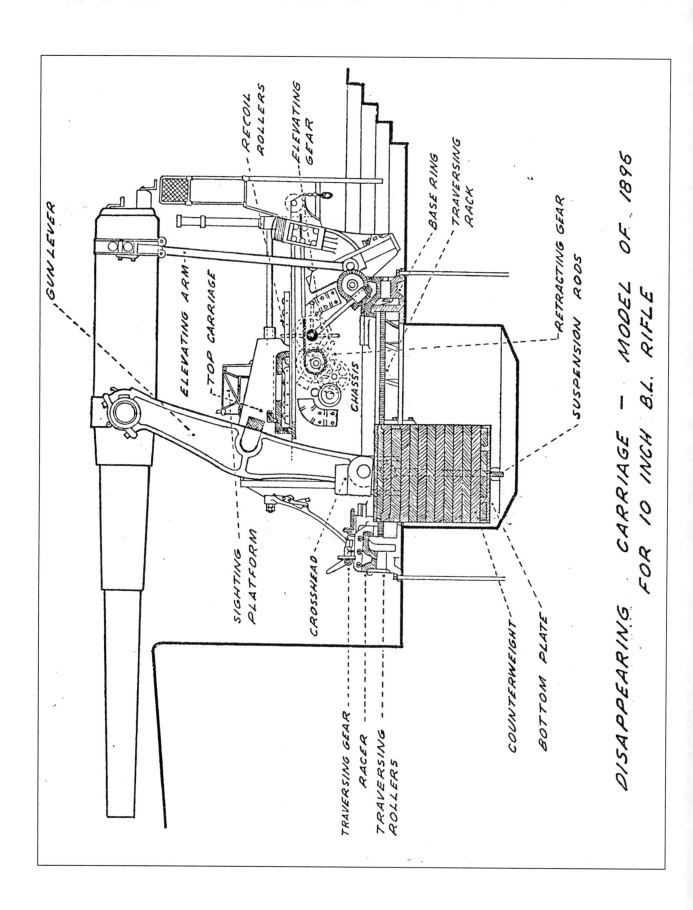

CHAPTER THREE

The Golden Age: 1900 - 1918

THE PROGRAM PRESENTED BY THE ENDICOTT BOARD IN 1886 CALLED FOR AN ENORMOUS EXPENDITURE of money on defensive fortifications. The recommendations were based largely on a study done immediately after the Civil War by a Board of Engineers and developments that had taken place during the last 10 years in armament, ordnance, and fortifications. The defensive system was radically different from defensive systems of earlier days in that it did not emphasize the fortification structures, but, instead the weapons contained therein.

The construction that began in 1897 was based primarily on the Endicott Board Report. Instead of high masonry walls, the new system was to rely on low profile, concrete and earthen emplacements spread over a much wider area than forts of the pre-Civil war days and designed to blend into the surrounding landscape as much as possible. A battery was usually two, three, or four semi-circular positions of concrete with the forward part left in its natural state so that nothing would be visible from the front at all. The emplacements were on two levels, the upper surface level carrying the gun and the lower level housing the magazines and power house. These were protected by a large layer of concrete and/or earth cover. Ammunition was supplied to the gun platform by vertical lifts to the flank traverse between guns. From here the shells and powder charges were taken by trolleys to the guns for loading.[1] The gun mountings were either barbette type, in which the gun barrel projected over the parapet, or disappearing type, in which the gun was raised and lowered below the level of the parapet to fire and reload.

The Board's program called for 26 coastal defensive sites and three on the Great Lakes, with turreted guns, armored cupolas, floating batteries, mines and about 1300 guns of 8-inch caliber and above. The cost was in excess of $126 million dollars.[2] The size and scope of the Board's program was unrealistic and in many cases the coastal defense works built did not come close to meeting the dimensions of the original plan. Nevertheless, the Board's proposal served as the basic framework for a new generation of seacoast defenses. As the Spanish-American War began, construction was in full swing in most localities and the golden age of Coastal Defense had begun. In the eighteen years after 1900, Fort Casey enjoyed a position of importance in the defense program of the United States and like the other forts of the Sound benefited greatly from this role.

At Fort Casey, there were three classes of armament used. The first consisted of three batteries of 10-inch rifles. These guns were flat-trajectory weapons that were limited to how high they could be angled upward. They were designed to shoot at the sides of attacking ships and though limited in their angle of elevation they had sufficient range to match or outshoot the guns of contemporary battleships. The 10- and 6-inch guns at Casey were mounted on the ingenious disappearing-type carriage. Originally developed in England; a primitive form of it was used as early as early as 1869. It was not until 1885, however, that the carriage system was perfected using a hydro-pneumatic system instead of the original hydraulic design to absorb the shock of firing and to raise and lower the gun.[3] The system was called the Moncrieff disappearing mounting, after the man who developed the design. In America the English version was considered inferior to what was designed by two U. S. Army ordnance officers, Adelbert R. Buffington and William Crozier. The American design permitted a greater rate of fire and allowed the guns to be elevated slightly higher. The American system was based on a counterweight principal rather than the more troublesome hydro-pneumatic system.[4]

The Buffington-Crozier carriage consisted essentially of a pair of massive lever arms to support

ABOVE: A 10″ Disappearing Rifle in the down or loading position at Battery Worth.

ABOVE: A 10″ Disappearing Rifle in the up or firing position at Battery Worth. Note that the catwalks and railings have not been installed yet in this picture.

LEFT: One of the two forward 12" mortar in the up or firing position at Battery Schenck.

BELOW: One of the two four gun mortar pits in Battery Schenck. Note the covers over the barrel openings. It was discovered by the troops that the standard Army garbage can lids perfectly fit the gun barrels of the mortars and could be effectively be used to seal them off from the weather.

the gun tube. Upon firing, the tube and the upper end of the arms were carried to the rear and downward by recoil energy, which at the same time raised a heavy lead counterweight attached to the opposite end of the arms from a well beneath the emplacement. Buffered by hydraulic cylinders, the gun descended below the level of the parapet until the breech was about three feet from the emplacement floor and positioned for loading. In this loading position, the gun was totally concealed from enemy sights and protected by earth and concrete against direct fire. The gun was held by a ratchet device on the counterweight while it was loaded. When loading was completed and ready to fire, the gun was 'tripped', that is, the counterweight was allowed to drop back into its well and, by turning the lever arms, carry the gun barrel back above the parapet.[5] This type of mounting, which made the guns all but invisible and invulnerable from the seaward direction, was used with 10-inch and 6-inch rifles at Fort Casey. Because the gun always returned to the loading position after firing, skilled gun crews could fire up to three shots a minute from the 10-inch. Considering the size of the weapon this was a remarkable feat.

The second class of armament used at Admiralty Head was the 12-inch mortar. These short, stubby weapons were usually installed in batteries of eight or sixteen. They were designed to lob their 700-pound projectiles in high arcs to come down almost vertically onto the lightly armored decks of ships. At Fort Casey, the mortars were built in clusters of four guns within a square, pit-like emplacement. They were on the reverse side of the hill onto which the fort was built. To be fired, the guns had to shoot over the top of the surrounding slopes and over the fort itself. Placed as they were, they were completely shielded from direct naval fire. The emplacements were a one-level design, with magazines and equipment contained within tunnels built into the high embankments surrounding the pits on three sides.

The third classification of armament at Fort Casey developed as a support for the larger guns were smaller rifles of 3-, 5-, and 6-inch caliber. The 6-inch rifles were mounted on disappearing carriages while the 5-inch guns were on balanced pillars and the 3-inch guns were on pedestal mounts. These weapons used ammunition light enough to be handled manually and could therefore be fired at a much quicker rate than the bigger weapons. They were designated as rapid-fire weapons and could, with trained crews, fire from five to fifteen rounds per minute.[6] Other than the 6-inch guns, these rapid-fire batteries were of simple design set into a rather plain concrete emplacement. They were designed with low surrounding parapets and adjacent protected magazines. Most were mounted behind steel shields for the protection of the men. Clustered in groups of two or four guns at various points around the fort, they provided covering fire for beaches and the dock area. They were also to provide secondary support fire for the main gun batteries.

As the construction proceeded at Admiralty Head, the fort continued to grow in size and manpower. The first two batteries of 10-inch rifles, Worth and Moore, and the 12-inch batteries of mortars, Seymour and Schenck, were finished by 1900 and work was already under way at the 5-inch emplacement, Battery Turman. The Spanish-American war in 1898 spurred further construction at Casey and the other harbor forts. On the drawing board projections were now being made for three more 10-inch gun emplacements and a host of new support buildings.

Early in 1901 there was a re-organization within the Army that was of direct relevance to harbor defense and Fort Casey. The reorganization created two separate and distinct branches of artillery in the Army. Before this time, both Coast and Field Artillery services were performed by the same regiments but as the weapons became more advanced, it required more specialized training to properly operate them. With the advent of rifled ordnance around 1890 the physical differences between field and seacoast artillery were multiplied even more. The two branches were developing their own tactics. The Field Artillery was oriented toward increasing mobility and better coordination with the infantry and cavalry; the Coast Defense was concerned with more technical matters such as ammunition handling, night-time harbor illumination and fire control.[7] It became too difficult for one arm of the army to handle it all, so in 1901 the branches were split. Coast Artillery and Field Artillery became separate with the creation of 126 companies of Coast Artillery and 30 batteries of Field Artillery. Each Coast Artillery Company was roughly of a size appropriate to the manning of either a major caliber gun or mortar battery, two or more rapid-fire batteries, or a mine battery.[8] With this change, the men serving coastal defense were given a new and more recognizable identity in the Army.[9]

New land for the fort reservation was acquired in 1901 and by 1902 the completed batteries of weapons were turned over to the first Coast Artillery Companies to arrive at Fort Casey. These men of the 63rd and 71st companies of Coast Artillery were but the first of many companies of men to be stationed at the fort during the first decade of the 1900's. During this decade, the fort was steadily undergoing changes in both personnel and appearance. New gun emplacements of 6- and 3-inch caliber were built, as were the majority of the fort's buildings. The first Battery Command stations were built by 1903 as was the new light house and the Fire Commanders Station. In 1904, a submarine cable was laid across the bottom of Admiralty Inlet by the Signal Corps and telephone communications between Forts Worden, Flagler, and Casey were completed. Portable electric searchlights were assigned to the fort for night identification of ships and voice tubes were installed at all the main emplacements to permit communication with men below the parapets and gun levels.[10]

Another event that was of some consequence was the appointment of the Taft Board in January of 1905. Set up by the energetic President Theodore Roosevelt, this board, headed by Secretary of War William H. Taft, was to examine port fortifications. Similar to the Endicott Boards work, the Taft Board was to review earlier programs and to bring them up to date. It had been twenty years since the Endicott recommendations, and a number of developments had taken place that required incorporation into the harbor defense system. The major changes brought about by the Taft Board's recommendations were not so much in armament or fortification structures as in the area of accessory harbor defense equipment.[11] Its proposals accelerated the installation of many features that had been projected for construction by the Endicott Board but had not as yet been installed. These new additions at Fort Casey included a modern aiming system for major caliber guns and mortars, electrical power plants, and permanent searchlight emplacements.

The new aiming system was the most significant advance to be made in harbor defense fire-control until the introduction of radar in World War II. Prior to this time, aiming was generally done by sighting the target through some form of telescope and then shooting. Hitting the target was largely the result of experience and a lot of luck. The new system, by comparison, was based on highly developed optical instruments and precise mathematical calculations. Targeting was based on two or more widely spaced sightings of the objective. Using an optical sighting instrument, the Lewis Depression Position Finder (DPF), sightings were made from base-end stations at different locations

ABOVE: Men of the 85th Company, Coast Artillery, waiting for chow in 1913.

BELOW: The Guard mount of the 12th Company Coast Artillery in dress uniforms.

ABOVE: The Fort Casey baseball team. Games on the parade grounds drew large crowds as the team was one of the best in the area.

BELOW: Jess Martin was one of the Fort Casey baseball team's best players or as the photo lists, a heavy hitter.

around the reservation. Each of the gun batteries had three separate sighting instruments designated to get firing information just for that particular set of guns. The primary stations were located in metal buildings on high ground to the rear of the main 10-inch batteries. Secondary observation stations, usually small concrete or wooden buildings housing the DPF instruments, were positioned at three locations: the northern end of the reservation, on the narrow strip of land south of Crockett's Lake and near the lighthouse. Distances between the primary and secondary optical stations varied from 500 to 2,500 yards.

These sighting or fire-control stations reported information about the target (direction moving, approximate distance, estimated speed, number of stacks) to the Battery Commander's Station. There the three separate sightings were triangulated on huge plotting boards that showed the Inlet and surroundings areas laid out in map form. Allowances were made and corrections worked in for meteorological factors and such other variables as target progress during the projectile time of flight and the time taken to figure all of this information out. The final figures were then transmitted by telephone to the gun batteries designated to fire.[12] This was an elaborate system but one that proved to be very precise and extremely accurate. The expertise of the gunners at Fort Casey and all the forts of the coastal defense were well known. Competitions were regularly held with other forts on the Pacific Coast and the gunners of Admiralty Inlet were among the best.

Plans for providing electricity at Fort Casey had been recommended as early as 1902. Almost all of the emplacements had electrical conduit channels built in when they were constructed and it had been more or less expected that a power plant of some kind would soon be built. Each year's annual report from the Corps of Engineers continually pointed out the need for permanent electrical power and the vulnerability of the fort to night attack. It was not until 1905, however, that the plans were finally begun.

Before this time, all lighting at Fort Casey was by oil lamps, including the gun emplacements. There really was no adequate way, other than lanterns, to illuminate the guns for night drills. Official reports show that the breakage rate of the emplacement lights went up dramatically whenever full service target practice was held. By mid-1910, the central power plant was finally completed and put into service the following year. Additional electrical power stations were constructed for the searchlight emplacements but these were of a much smaller nature. By 1911, most of Fort Casey had electricity.[13]

The building of the power plant not only brought light to the emplacements, but helped to provide the means to illuminate the waters of Admiralty Inlet at night. Power, partially provided by the smaller individual generator stations, was now available for five permanent searchlights which were built and turned over to the Coast Artillery in April of 1911. These powerful, 60-inch, carbon-arc lights were designed to provide nighttime illumination of the harbor entrances. When turned on they could easily shine the three miles across the Inlet and on more than one occasion created daytime in the middle of the night for local residents in Port Townsend.

The tactical lights, as they were officially designated, were located at three locations on the post. The first two were on the bluff at the north end of the reservation, the second two on the bluff below the main 10-inch emplacements, and the last one was placed well out on the spit along Crockett's Lake. Searchlight #12, out on the spit, was installed atop a 25 foot wooden tower to give it maximum advantage for spotting within the Inlet.

All the forts of the Coastal Defense benefited from the Taft Board's recommendations for improvements. The other services were also being transformed in the first decade of the 1900s. The United States' leaders now believed that the nation possessed a wealth and a military potential that could draw her into international political activity whether she willed it or not. To meet this new challenge, they argued a strengthening of the military services, and in particular, a strong Navy.

During these first years of the twentieth century more and more Americans were becoming believers in the new doctrine of "Manifest Destiny." While the old concept of "manifest destiny" had sped the conquest/settlement of California and Oregon and was based on the superiority of the American people and democracy, the new doctrine, which was revived in the late nineteenth century, was now ornamented with fashionable ideas and scientific notions. The Imperialists, those people wanting to expand America by going beyond the continental borders, looked to Darwinism for support. They looked to "natural selection," as a defense for their conquest of "natives" and "backward peoples" in tropical climates.[14] The Hawaiian Islands, the Philippines, Cuba, and the South Pacific islands all fit nicely into this category. Those who had the might and ability to do so were the fittest to rule. There was now a race to secure these far flung outposts and extend the security of the nation. Unfortunately this could hardly be accomplished with a small antiquated Navy.

Along with these concepts, other ideas grew about the new role the country should take in international politics. The writings of Alfred T. Mahan on the building of a strong, offense-oriented navy, the experience of the Spanish-American War, and the awareness of the rising ambitions and power in Germany and Japan were persuading a small but influential minority of Americans of the importance of naval preparedness. Men like Theodore Roosevelt, Elihu Root and Senator Henry Cabot Lodge, among others believed it important that the United States operate from a position of strength. Every powerful nation, in their view, had a stake in the world order and a responsibility to preserve it.

Roosevelt, as president, demanded the construction of a modern Navy. Before he left office in 1909, the Navy's effectiveness had been doubled. Both the Army and the Navy profited from the enthusiastic recognition the President gave to the military and the increased percentage of the Federal Budget that now was directed toward the services. Secretary of War Root also urged that the preparedness of the nation be given more attention. Root proposed that the reinforcement, equipment and operation of a war time Army be planned as much as possible during times of peace. This new attention to the military services brought new Congressional appropriations and renewed interest in advanced technology. The new Coast Artillery also benefited from this growth.[15]

A fundamental change was taking place also, in the relationship between the harbor defenses and the Navy. Since the days of George Washington, the Navy had been tied to coastal defense, and, in theory, commerce raiding. These views had changed very little by the 1880s and consequently more attention had been paid to maintaining a fleet for defensive purposes. Because of this the Navy had been allowed to deteriorate into an obsolete and antiquated collection of wooden ships and floating batteries that provoked foreign ridicule.[16]

The exact definition of what constituted the Navy's role in coast defense had never been well defined. Some saw it as a mere extension of harbor defense; others saw it as a means to defend the long stretches of unfortified coastline; still others saw it as a less expensive substitute for fortifications. Whatever the view, it was generally agreed that the Navy was to operate the same as fortifications. This

ABOVE: A hunting party bringing back fresh meat for the men of their barracks.

BELOW: Now it was the job of the barrack's cooks to prepare the food for the men.

ABOVE: Raising of the flag on the parade ground and the firing of the ceremonial field piece. Officer's row is in the background and the Commanding Officers quarters is on the end.

BELOW: Field meet between the men of Forts Worden, Flagler, and Casey on the parade grounds at Fort Worden.

unmistakable emphasis on the Navy's passive defense role was reflected in a succession of ponderous, heavy gunned, but often unseaworthy ships, many of them experimental only, which included Fulton's *Demologous* of 1814, the various pre-1860 steam batteries, the monitors, retained long after the Civil War, the floating batteries proposed by the Endicott Board, and the so-called "sea-going coastal battleships" of the 1890s.[17]

With America's emergence into world affairs some argued that the Navy could no longer remain defensive. There were certain officers who tried, unsuccessfully, to win release for the Navy from its passive defensive role. It was not until the 1890s, however, that the role of the Navy as an offensive weapon, free from the shackles of coast defense, was publicly expressed. No one was more aware of the Navy's deficiencies and what its potential could be than Captain Alfred T. Mahan. Instead of defense, he stressed offense and his command-of-the-seas concept gained widespread circulation. Mahan wrote in 1890: "Whether they will or no, Americans must now begin to look outward."[18]

The reawakening of American expansionism overseas, the war with Spain, the writings of Mahan and Theodore Roosevelt's popularization of Mahan's concepts; all worked to fundamentally change the Navy. Passive coast defense doctrine was eliminated; the connection with seacoast defenses was broken. In addressing a conference at the Naval War College early in 1908, Roosevelt left no doubt as to the completeness of the transformation or to the new role to be taken by the Coastal Defense. He stated:

> *Let the port be protected by the Army's fortifications; the fleet must be foot-loose to search out and destroy the enemy's fleet; that is the function of the fleet... For the protection of our coasts we need fortifications; not merely to protect the salient points of our possessions, but we need them so that the Navy can be foot-loose.*[19]

Harbor Defense forts throughout the country continued to increase in manpower and armament. By 1910 many of the installations were approaching the original projections made by the Endicott Board which had been considered too costly to ever build. Puget Sound had been enlarged to such an extent that it ranked as the fourth most strongly fortified point in the United States, after New York, San Francisco, and Boston.[20]

Since this was the period before the airplane and the U-boat, the basic American military doctrine for coast artillery became protection from invasion. That was considered the only real threat to the nation. Such an invasion would require the capture of a seaport since a land invasion anywhere else would allow time for garrisoned troops to be brought up to fight. With forts guarding these ports, like the ones at Admiralty Inlet, such invasions would be extremely costly if not impossible. Because it was essential in the defense plans, a large part of the Army's strength was allocated to the Coast Artillery Corps. During some years before World War I, one fourth of the Army's total strength and one third of all troops in the United States were composed of Coast Artillerymen.[21] By 1912, there were three companies stationed at Fort Casey: the 71st & 149th, consisting of 103 enlisted men each, and the 85th, with 102 enlisted men.[22]

The political problems in Europe and this new awareness in the growing potential of the American military led to continued increases in manpower and improvements at all the forts in the Puget Sound.

Work was completed on two new forts in the Sound. Fort Whitman, located on Goat Island, and Fort Ward at Bean Point were added to the defense system. Additional fire control stations were being added at Fort Casey, as well as the continuous training of the stationed troops. Inspections of the forts, however, showed that deficiencies still left the installations vulnerable. A report on the preparedness of the Pacific Coast Artillery, dated June 30, 1913, pointed out a great many problems to the commanding General of the Western Department. The following deficiencies were listed for Fort Casey:

1. *Low supply of ammunition at the fort; Estimated that continuous fire could only be kept up for 8 minutes.*

2. *The fort was still not fully lighted; Battery Parker in particular was without electricity.*

3. *The phone system was not yet completed to all branches of the fort, particularly plotting rooms.*

4. *The problems of mining the Inlet had still not been solved. More experimentation was called for.*

5. *Leaks in the 10-inch magazines were becoming a real concern. Just about all leaked and badly!*

6. *The lack of authorized company strength at the fort. Casey should have had 11 companies totaling close to 2,000 enlisted men. At this time Casey had 3 companies.*

7. *Battery Turman: in wrong place and not needed. It was felt the battery blocked the Fire-Control Center by the light house and its guns could be put to better use at Fort Ward.*

CONCLUSION: *Coast Artillery District is not in as satisfactory a condition as regards preparedness as it should be.*[23]

Some of these problems would be remedied fairly quickly but others would still be present at the beginning of World War I. Manpower, in particular, never did reach authorized levels.

Daily life at the army post was pretty dull. Coupeville was the closest town, (population under 500), and was not exactly a thriving center of activities. Through the early part of the 1900s, as the fort was being built up both in facilities and personnel, the soldiers at the 'Rock', as it was called, had little in the way of outside entertainment. Along with the building of the gun emplacements and the temporary living quarters, a small baseball diamond was put in on the hill. Baseball became a favorite pastime of the enlisted men and games against teams from the other forts were fairly common. Occasionally, there was a ball in Port Townsend, but this was limited to officers and only then if the weather permitted the small army tender to cross the Inlet to pick them up.

Other than baseball and the solitude of a walk on the beach, about the only other outlet for the soldiers at the fort were visits to nearby saloons. The sale of alcohol was not permitted on the military reservation but this did not stop enterprising businessmen from locating their establishments within spitting distance of the post gates. With the fairly large numbers of workers and soldiers, this appears to have been a golden period for tavern owners. There were three saloons located within easy walking distance of the fort. One in particular was located just across Crockett's Lake on the Chicago Beach.

ABOVE: The completed Fort Casey Lighthouse in 1909. Note the mule barn on the far right and how much of the trees in the immediate vicinity had been cleared away. The second lighthouse to be constructed at Admiralty Head began in 1902 and was completed by 1903. This considerably more substantial brick structure is still standing.

In the late 1890s, enthusiastic real estate investors had speculated that a new community would develop along the beach below the fort. The spit running south from where the Engineer's Wharf and the Quartermaster's Dock were located was to be developed into a new city on the Sound. Names like New Brooklyn and Little Chicago were used in referring to different sections along the beach. A boom of sorts occurred and a number of buildings and a wooden bridge across Crockett's Lake were built. Of course, among the buildings erected were a number of saloons. It was at one of these saloons, 'The Stump,' owned by a Frank Grove, that an unfortunate incident took place. On the evening of December 8th, 1904, a worker at the fort, John Dollar, who had apparently stopped in to just buy a cigar was killed by a gunshot to the head. A number of shots were fired into the saloon, and eventually a post soldier and a civilian were arrested by the local sheriff. The next evening an inquest was held with a coroner and a jury of six civilians. The following account of the inquest is given:

At the inquest it was noted that owner Groves was surly and not inclined to admit that his tavern was anything but a genteel social club.

Q. How did the window get broke?

A. Someone went through it.

Q. Do you ever break up chairs or tables in your janglings here?

A. Not any more than is usual in a saloon.

Q. Didn't you have a regular row here two or three weeks ago?

A. No. No more than is usual in a saloon. Never have any more roughhouse than any saloon--not what I call roughhouse.

The soldiers who were questioned described sinister civilians who were lurking at the bar that night. The civilians were equally sure that a treacherous soldier had fired the shots.[24]

Soldiers who had been in the saloon were interrogated but none could shed any light as to who fired the fatal shots or for that matter how they managed to get across the Crockett's Lake Bridge to the fort. The guard on duty at the bridge claimed to have passed civilians but no soldiers after the shots were fired but the fact remained that the troops who had been in the saloon made it back to the fort.

Life could be dangerous even in somewhat isolated places. Both the soldier and the civilian were released, and no punishment was ever inflicted as far as John Dollar was concerned. Several civilian workers at the fort were disciplined for frequenting such places. All were warned to stay away.

The fort continued to grow in the years leading up to World War I. By 1910, the fort was considered the best town on the island. Many of the officers and NCOs had their families living at the base with them or in the Coupeville area. Children were provided transportation into town via horse drawn wagon to attend school and there were many community/fort social events. The fort had a parade ground with a regulation sized baseball diamond. There was a bakery, a tailor shop, a post exchange, a quartermaster building, a telephone office, and a number of new recreational facilities. A three-hole golf course was located just below the commanding officers quarters at the far end of the parade ground. A gym with facilities for basketball and other indoor activities was built. It also had a bowling alley in the basement. A tennis court was installed as well as a base show house.[25]

Training for the soldiers stationed at the fort was a daily routine. They were instructed both in the skills of a regular soldier as well as in the use of artillery of all calibers. The guns at the fort were fired regularly in target practice and the fort participated in yearly war game drills. It should be noted that the guns were not fired with full service ammunition very often. Because of the cost of the powder, shells and the wear and tear on the gun barrels, sub-caliber ammunition was used a good deal of the time. Smaller gun tubes were installed within or on top of the regular barrel so that smaller caliber or sub-caliber ammunition could be used and the original barrel saved. For example, a 3-inch barrel could be fitted into the 10-inch rifles and then 3-inch shells were fired from the gun. In the 3-inch rapid-fire guns 50 caliber machine guns were fitted. In this way the soldiers were able to practice with the actual guns but did not wear them out as fast or shoot up as much expensive ammunition.[26]

On certain occasions, the forts of the Sound participated in simulated attacks in joint drills with the regular Army. The men were kept at war alert for 24 hours at a time to simulate night attacks and everything dealing with actual wartime activities. They were trained in all aspects of gunnery from small arms to the large caliber rifles. Gunnery records testify to the quality of marksmanship shown by the Casey soldiers by the number of blue ribbons awarded for accuracy and organization. It took teamwork to fire the 10-inch disappearing rifles or the 12-inch mortars, from the target spotters to the plotting room to the gun crew. Each gun battery competed not only against other batteries of the fort, but also against batteries from Worden and Flagler. Competition was keen, as in some cases, superiority in firing accuracy over other batteries could mean more pay. At various times between 1903 and 1910, gunners from each of the three Admiralty Inlet forts won regimental honors for marksmanship.[27]

When target practice was held for the gunners, one of the Coast Artillery mine planters or smaller launches would tow a target through the inlet. A raft was built, and onto this was erected a rectangular frame 60 feet long and 30 feet high. This was covered in a fine net and pulled by a boat on a tow rope about 1,000 feet long. The target was designed to be 1/5th the dimension of a battleship and had to be actually penetrated to record a hit. Many of the Engineer's records show that on target practice days, not all guns got their turn to fire, as the target would be destroyed by earlier shells-in many cases, in as few as 10 shots.[28]

In 1916 an unfortunate incident occurred during a practice firing that illustrated the power of the huge weapons. In this case Company 8 of the State Militia, during summer maneuvers at Fort Flagler, was operating the 12-inch mortars in Battery Bankhead. A target was being towed through the strait by the launch, *General Wilson*. The crew received orders to commence firing. The shots boomed across the waters and the target was destroyed. The gun crews were ordered to continue going through a dry run. The SOP (standing operating procedure) called for a practice shell. Instead, a heavy shell was slammed into the breech and the live powder charge slipped in behind it. "Commence firing!" was ordered. The 125-pound projectile arced out into the Sound and plummeted down the smokestack of the towing ship. The shell went through the keel of the boat and disappeared as did the *General Wilson* in short order. Apparently all hands escaped before the boat sank.[29]

There were other incidents of the misfiring of these large guns in the relatively limited space of Admiralty Inlet. One in particular happened near Ebbey's Landing on Whidbey Island, where a local farmer was plowing his field. He heard a whistling sound and was utterly shocked when a 10-inch dummy shell landed nearby. He recovered enough from the shock to dig up the dummy shell that had been fired from Fort Flagler and put it on exhibition in the nearby Coupeville Hotel.

The assassination at Sarajevo in 1914 heightened the anxiety at Fort Casey and the other forts of the Sound over possible United States involvement in European problems but did little else. The men were aware of the fighting going on in Europe, but only from reports appearing in local newspapers. As the First World War began, the troops continued to train and the forts continued to improve. Plotting rooms were built during 1914-1915 for each of the 10-inch rifle and 12-inch mortar batteries. This would enable them to react more swiftly to target information and free the Fire Command Headquarters from so much coordination and individual plotting. Additional target spotting stations were installed and in general there was a constant upgrading of the whole fire control system during these years.

The first hints of impending American involvement came late in 1915 but was unknown by those at Fort Casey. A letter was sent from Lieutenant Colonel E. Eveleth Winslow, Corps of Engineers, to the Chief of Engineers in Seattle. The letter made a strong recommendation of the need for 3-inch antiaircraft guns at the fort. It seemed that Lieutenant Colonel Winslow was concerned with the potentially dangerous role the airplane could play in an attack on the forts on Puget Sound.[30] He was not alone in his worries, as many military leaders were concerned with the role that air ships, planes as well as dirigibles, were taking in the War in Europe. Congress first recognized the need for some sort of air defense before the War in 1913. During Congressional hearings the potential dangers of an attack from enemy aeroplanes was described quite vividly by Brigadier General George P. Scriven, Chief Signal Officer of the Army. Questions were raised as to what weapons the Army had to defend against the airplane. Brigadier General Scriven informed the hearings Chairman that experiments were being carried out, but he did not know of any developments.[31]

At the time, the Army was more concerned with dirigibles than airplanes. After the start of the War, more interest was expressed concerning the need for weapons that could be elevated higher and could fire much quicker than conventional ordnance. It was not until 1915, however, that something was actually done. In that year a 3-inch antiaircraft gun project belatedly got under way. It is not clear if Lieutenant Colonel Winslow knew of this project when he wrote his letter but technical journals of the day were discussing it and the role of aerial warfare more and more as the War in Europe progressed and the air plane took a more prominent role. It would seem unlikely that Winslow would make such a suggestion to the chief of Engineers without some knowledge of the Army experiments. In any event, the letter was filed and apparently forgotten, at least for the time being.

As the war in Europe staggered into 1916, the world at Fort Casey continued in its ordered and disciplined way. The children of the fort personnel were taken to school in Coupeville and the bakery wagon continued to bring fresh baked bread up to the men at the emplacements and to the barracks each day. New companies of soldiers were brought in as were National Guard troops for occasional training.

Christmas dinner in 1916 was served to soldiers and civilians who worked at Fort Casey courtesy of the 2nd Company Coast Artillery Corps. Some of those present at this annual affair must have suspected that war was coming but for them the biggest problem was finding room for the sumptuous meal that was served. The menu is to look at and envy!

MENU
2ND CO. C. A. C., FORT CASEY
CHRISTMAS 1916

Turkey Soup   *Oysters Crackers*

Roast Turkey a la Maryland   *Roast Loin of Pork*

Baked Halibut   *Cranberry Sauce*

Giblet Dressing   *Bechamel Sauce*

Candied Sweet Potatoes   *Mashed Potatoes*

Creamed Sweet   *Peas Creamed*   *Sweet Corn*

Lobster Salad

Celery   *Chow Chow*   *Sweet Pickles*

Olives

Layer Cake   *Ribbon Cake*   *English Plum Duff*

Brandy Sauce   *Meringue Lemon Pie*   *Mince Pie*

Oranges   *Apples*   *Bananas*

Nuts   *Mixed Candy*

Bread   *Butter*   *Cocoa*

Cigars[32]

RIGHT: Two members of the Washington National Guard during their assigned stay at Fort Casey. Their training in a wide variety of heavy weapons and artillery as well as all the standard training of the regular Army turned them into some of the best trained troops to be sent to Europe.

BELOW: The soldiers field kit that all were expected to carry with them into battle. From the left: tent pegs, waterproof tarp, eating utensils, canteen, ammunition belt, and pack.

CHAPTER FOUR

WORLD WAR I AT FORT CASEY

With the American entry into World War I in April of 1917, activity again was stepped up at Fort Casey. New companies of men were transferred in and in some small way the men of the Coast Artillery were perhaps more prepared for war than the rest of the services. As early as 1915, a vocal minority began preaching the need for the country to prepare. The President was mindful of the coming election and how important the political issue of preparedness had become. Wilson instructed the armed services to plan for expansion but the quotas that were proposed were never reached. All of the services, including Coast Defense, continually fought to obtain the men needed, not just for preparedness, but necessary for the basic manning of the weapons.

Forts, like Casey and the others of Admiralty Inlet, grew. New emplacements were built, enlarged, and new weapons were added without a real consideration for the staffing needs to properly man the fortifications. As early as 1908 the Secretary of War, Luke E. Wright, described the problem.

> *Without an adequate force of trained men . . . our seacoast fortifications are useless and all the expenditures made upon time . . . are worse than wasted, for they have lured us into a false sense of security and protection.*[1]

In the years leading up to World War I the Coast Artillery was both an essential branch of the Army and a formidable weapon in defense of our nation but it was continually undermanned. Our defenses were strong. Those troops that were there could do their jobs very well. Their abilities, however, did not make up for the fact that many of the gun batteries did not have enough crews manning them. The manpower need of coast defense was a fixed quantity based upon the catalog of guns, mortars, and other appliances in the fortifications. The figure was precise. Any amount more would be a waste of manpower. Unlike the cavalry or infantry, the coast artillery did not become more menacing as it acquired more personnel. What mattered most were the weapons in place and how many of them had complete manning details.[2]

Trying to steer a middle-of-the-road course, President Wilson supported Congressional measures to accelerate the building of the Navy that Roosevelt had begun and the doubling of the regular Army. These measures satisfied the majority of Americans but were not enough to prepare the nation or the military for the coming conflict. To properly man the Coast Artillery fortifications that had been constructed since 1900 would have required a force then almost equal to the entire standing army

The country and particularly the armed services were unprepared when the nation entered the war. Some progress had been made but these fell far short of what had been called for or would be needed. One military expert summed up the nation's shortcomings by stating that on April 6, 1917, when Congress responded to President Wilson's War message, the United States Army was less ready for the task ahead of it than at the opening of any previous conflict, not excepting the War of the Revolution or the War of 1812.[3] This may be too strong an assessment of the Army but can easily be applied to the nation as a whole. Unfortunately this same bleak description would be repeated some 24 years later after a fateful Sunday in Hawaii.

Six weeks before his War message, Wilson had called most of the National Guard into federal service, under the terms of the new National Defense Act, and these men were now to play a major role

ABOVE: A group of National Guardsmen fully armed and ready for action outside their tent behind the main emplacements. They were still living in the tents as the temporary or Cantonment buildings were not completed as yet. The Regular Army troops occupied the main barracks.

BELOW: The troops did manage to have some free time from their training. Here a friendly gambling activity takes place obviously outside the view of any officers.

ABOVE: Troops of the 85th C.A.C. in full service practice firing of gun #1 in Battery Kingsbury. Notice the gun tube at the bottom of the picture. This was the gun tube from #2 Kingsbury and had been removed in 1909 for reasons not defined. Gun tube #1 was removed in 1918 for scrap, but #2 was kept in the area. It was remounted in 1920 as it was the only heavy weapon at any of the three Admiralty Inlet forts that was capable of shooting at the inner harbor should an enemy ship get past the forts.

RIGHT: Target practice in Admiralty Inlet. The 60' tall target was towed by an Army mine planter stationed at Fort Worden.

concerning Coastal Defense. One of the Army's most urgent needs, besides manpower, was for heavy artillery to employ in France. The Coast Artillery branch was now to perform the duty of training the nation and the military for the coming conflict.

The first troops in Washington to respond to the national call up were the state militia or National Guard. These men had some basic training and many had participated in two week training sessions at Fort Worden. These newly drafted guardsmen began to arrive at Fort Casey and the other posts of the Sound in the latter part of 1917. They were immediately mustered into the Coast Artillery upon arrival and began their training. Until national conscription began to take affect, the Washington National Guard troops would man the coast defense. Unprepared for service as they were, their situation was made worse when the majority of regular Army men were removed for overseas duty. It was now up to a skeleton force of non-commissioned officers to train the men.

Two of these National Guardsmen who reported to Fort Casey in July of 1917 were Jess VanDemark and Henry Juvet. Both were 18 year olds from the Ferndale area who went from drilling on the grass fields at Bellingham Normal School (Western Washington University) to being mustered into the 63rd Company Coast Artillery. Jess VanDemark remembers:

> *About 30 of us traveled by car from Bellingham, took the ferry at Deception Pass, and arrived at Casey on July 25th. When we got there we were split up into Battery D of the 63rd and the rest into Battery F of the 65th Company. The regular army troops were living in the three main barracks and the cantonment barracks were still under construction so we lived in tents immediately behind the main batteries. We spent a good deal of our first weeks there helping with the construction.*[4]

One of the regular Army non-commissioned officers left at Casey to train the new recruits was Sergeant Frank Thesenvitz. He had been transferred to Fort Casey from Worden in 1916 and had been assigned to observation. From there he became an ordinance instructor and finally a gun commander at Battery Van Horne. As the national guardsmen began to arrive Thesenvitz recognized the problems he and the other regular Army troops were facing.

> *A good description of these new men at the time was "They arrived with only their oaths of enlistment and the general training orders issued to the forts." There were many who were in poor condition physically, as well as ignorant. They were generally farmers who had no background whatsoever in gunnery. Many had to be instructed in even the basic skills of gun handling and could only be given blank ammunition at first for fear of one of them shooting themselves. Another problem was the lack of proper clothing due to rationing. In these early months many soldiers at the post were forced to wear worn out shoes or thin tropical type clothing. The threat of an attack also added to the tension at the fort.*[5]

The division between the regular Army troops and the National Guard would continue throughout VanDemark and Juvets eleven month stay at Casey. They never would get to live in the main barracks but would occupy the newly build cantonment barracks by the lighthouse. They may have been under regular Army training but all their drilling and details were totally separate from them. They had their own mess halls, activities, and training on the guns. Each of the gun batteries had three separate gun crews that trained at different times under their own noncoms. One was made up of Regular Army, one was National Guard troops, and a third would eventually be made up of AEF (American Expeditionary Force) draftees. Henry Juvet remembers that there was definitely no love loss between the Regular Army troops and the civilian soldiers.

> *The regular Army and the Nationalized National Guard troops didn't mix much. In fact they didn't get along too well at all. They didn't consider us real soldiers. At one of our field days when we had competitions with them the tug-of-war teams ended up in a brawl out in the middle of the field. There was a lot of name calling on both sides.*[6]

Juvets first assignment was at Battery Worth as a powder monkey. His job was to place the large silk sacks of powder onto the carts to be pushed to the breech of the 10-inch disappearing rifle. Each of the sacks was two feet long, about 8" to 10" wide, and weighed about 90 pounds. It took two bags for each firing of the huge guns. The sacks were brought up from the magazines below the emplacements by elevator and then placed on the carts. He had especially vivid memories about the first time the big 10" rifles were fired with full load ammunition when he was present.

> *We followed out training and loaded the gun, everyone cleared the piece and we assumed our firing positions. You stood on your tip toes (so you wouldn't be knocked over by the concussion), opened your mouth (to equalize the pressure) and covered your ears. The lanyard was pulled and the gun fired. Unfortunately all the slow burning powder didn't burn up and it was spit out of the barrel after the shell left. It kept burning and it set the brush on the embankment in front of the gun emplacement on fire. The officers up on the top of the emplacement began yelling at us to all come up and help fight the fire. The whole hillside was burning.*[7]

These full load firings didn't happen that often as it would wear out the weapons as well as use up very expensive ammunition. In most cases training was done with sub-caliber firing. Smaller barrels would be fitted either inside or on the top of the larger weapons. In this way all the basic fundamentals of observing, tracking, and firing at a potential enemy vessel could be practiced without the wear and tear on the gun. This practice went on daily for all the gun crews as a part of their basic training. One of Henry Juvets more unusual duties while assigned to Battery Worth was as a powder re-mixer.

> *They took a bunch of us to this building where a canvas tarp was spread out in the middle of the room. Each of us was searched by the Sergeant to make sure no one had any cigarettes, matches or were wearing hobnailed boots, they didn't want us to blow the place up. We then all got into a circle. They gave each of us a bag of powder some of it new and some of it old. They had to have different ages of powder as it had to do with the burning rate when the guns were fired. The powder was in chunks about 2 inches long and as big around your finger. This was the slow burning powder that would provide explosive push all the way for the shell traveling down the barrel. We stood in this circle and when called on each would throw out a handful onto the center of the canvas. They had to blend it that way*

ABOVE: One of the 12" mortars has just been fired from pit #1 Battery Schenck. The shell can be seen at the top of the picture. Note the effect of the concussion of the banks of the emplacement.

LEFT: One of the 60" carbon arc searchlights located on the bluff below Battery Kingsbury. The rail system used to move the huge lights out to the end of the emplacement can be seen at the bottom.

LEFT: One of the new constructed Cantonment barracks built for the flood of new troops that began arriving at Fort Casey after the start of World War I. Located behind the light house, these buildings housed the National Guard Troops and eventually the AEF draftees.

BELOW: One of the mortar pits at Fort Casey probably Battery Seymour. This is a good example of the very confined nature of the pits at Casey. The pits at Fort Worden and Flagler were much larger in design to provide more room for the gun crews.

depending upon what kind of shell it was intended for. It was different for practice shells and the real ammunition. Eventually it would be repacked in silk sacks for firing. There were times when we even loaded our own shells. It was kind of like a pile driver pushing the explosive down into the shell case but that really bothered me so I avoided that detail.[8]

The training of the National Guard troops and the new conscripts that soon began arriving continued day after day. This training as regular soldiers as well as trained artillerymen was totally new for just about all of them. Sergeant Thesentitz remembered them as ignorant, but patriotic and dedicated to doing their duty. *"They may have been uneducated but they were there to serve their country and they were going to give their all. Some were so serious that they cried because they could not read."*[9] Totally foreign to the complexities of Coast Artillery as they were, the men persisted and learned how to accurately fire guns of all calibers. They overcame their enormous handicaps and learned so well that they formed into highly effective companies and were considered one of the best posts in the area.[10]

Private Juvet remained at Battery Worth until he was transferred to the 3" rapid fire guns at Battery Van Horne. He recalled training on the smaller weapon.

This was an easier gun to fire because it was so much smaller but worse because of the sound. The 10" guns were a big boom but these guns had more of a sharp crack and hurt your ears even worse. The big guns had more pressure but didn't hurt as much. On these guns I was a loader. The 3" shells were passed by hand up to the gunners from the magazines down below. There were 7 of us for each of the two guns with a Sergeant in charge. Every morning we would practice firing the gun 25 times. We would insert a sub-caliber barrel into the gun tube and fire Crag shells. These were the size of rifle shells. We would shoot at sea gulls or driftwood floating in the water near the beach. We killed quite a few sea gulls.[11]

So proficient did these men become that it is said they could knock sea gulls off logs at 300 yards with the big 10-inch guns. The excellence of their training was evident when troops from the Coast Artillery were shipped out during World War I. The men from Fort Casey showed themselves to be better trained as both gunners and infantrymen than the average soldiers wherever they were sent.[12]

The daily training the men at Casey went through was to prepare them for later service wherever they might be stationed. An average day at the fort was something like:

Reveille at 6:45
Breakfast at 7:30
After breakfast: a general policing of quarters and then exercise or calisthenics period.
Two hours of gunnery practice, dry run drills or sub-caliber firing.
Lunch was at 12:00
After lunch: drilling in Infantry tactics. In the winter classes in ordnance, ballistics and other fields pertaining to artillery.[13]

Private Juvet also remembered the other National Guard troops spending a lot of time working on the guns themselves.

> *In the afternoon after about four hours of drills in smaller weapons use or other drills we would all go up to the big guns. We would spend hours scrubbing, cleaning, polishing and greasing the guns as well as the decks around the guns. One day when the parapet apron around the 10" guns was particularly dirty from the Cosmoline and other grease, the Sergeant decided to have the area cleaned so he made up a lye solution. It was put on the cement and then washed down. Unfortunately it was so acidic that it ate through the soles of my shoes. I had brought these shoes with me from civilian life and when they were ruined I had nothing to wear. I went to the Sergeant for new shoes but they didn't have any. I had to cut out cardboard every day and put it inside my shoes before I went on duty. When I finally did get a new pair of shoes they were size 11 and I wear a size 9 ½. I wore these oversized shoes till we got our hobnail boots before we went overseas.*[14]

The supply problem the troops at the fort had to deal with was just another result of the lack of preparedness. Some of the troops were still wearing cotton uniforms even during winter while others had the heavy wool. A few of the troops were forced to wear old turn of the century dress uniforms for lack of anything else to wear. The standard rifle issue for the men was the 305. Springfield Model 1903 but some of the men were still being issued the 1895 Lee Enfield. There were even a number of Spanish-American field pieces with wagons and caissons at the post. Henry Juvet was there when they were test fired. "*I got to pull the firing lanyard but they cleared everyone else on the firing crew out because they didn't know what was going to happen. They might have exploded.*"[15] Shortages in men and materials would continue throughout 1917. Eventually even guns from the emplacements would be cannibalized to help in the war effort overseas.

During the war the character of the fort began to change. Due to the rationing in the country and rather low allotment of 12¢ per day, per man, at the post, every available section of land on the reservation was cultivated. Crops of wheat, corn, and oats were grown behind the batteries; livestock was raised wherever possible. What had been barren grass fields at the fort were now covered with wheat, and there were great numbers of sheep, pigs, and cattle. All were raised for food to increase the men's rations.[16]

New conscripts continued to pour into the fort for training, which caused considerable overcrowding. These men were forced to live in tents while the National Guard troops occupied the newly constructed cantonment barracks. The parade ground was covered with rows of canvas coverings, as were sections of the mortar batteries and anywhere else there was room. Other new buildings were also added to the facilities at Casey. A new hospital ward was built, along with two 66-man barracks, a mess hall, latrine, and two officer's quarters.[17] All of this construction took place during the later part of 1917 and in one great rush. Close to 1,000 men were now stationed at Fort Casey, but the number would slowly begin to decrease as the war progressed.

The War was, however, changing more than just the physical appearance of Fort Casey; it was creating a whole new way of life from preceding years. Advances in technology were making many of the fort's guns obsolete. New developments in naval gunnery now enabled ships to elevate their

ABOVE: Constant training on the big 10-inch disappearing rifles was a vital part of the education of all the Coast Artillery Troops at Fort Casey. Here men watch the loading process from atop the emplacement.

BELOW: A 6-inch disappearing rifle at Battery Valleau in the down or loading position. The doorway on the far left leads to the magazine.

guns to much higher elevations. With this change, guns of equal or greater size as those at the harbor forts could now shoot much greater distances and the intricate and costly disappearing carriages were no longer an advantage. The most damaging change was the advent of the airplane and its potential for bringing war from the sky. The openness that had once been an advantage to coast defense now became its greatest weakness. The gun batteries and their crews were totally exposed to aerial attack and there was really nothing that could be done about it. By the latter part of 1917 troops at the fort commenced dismounting the 6-inch guns of Battery Valleau. They were to be cut up and sold for scrap. Dismounting weapons at Batteries Parker, Turman, and Schenck would soon follow.

Corporal Jess VanDemark and Private Henry Juvet stayed at Fort Casey for just under eleven months. In June of 1918 they were part of the 63rd Coast Artillery that departed Fort Worden by ship for Seattle. From there they would cross the country by train and eventually would arrive at New York. Exactly one month from the date of departure from Fort Worden they would begin their Atlantic crossing and ultimately the fields of France.[18] They and the rest of the men of the 63rd thankfully were spared the horrors of battle as the war ended on November 11, 1918 before they were sent into action.

Sergeant Frank Thesenvitz remained stationed at Fort Casey throughout the war and beyond. As is the pattern after most wars, appropriations and money for care and maintenance disappeared and all the elaborate plans and pronouncements for preparedness were forgotten in the euphoria of peace. He watched as the fort and coast defense was slowly allowed to sink into neglect and disrepair. He would leave Admiralty Head for good in 1927.

This period, from roughly 1900 to 1918, was one of progress and expansion for at that time the Coast Artillery was one of the most dynamic and technically advanced branches of the Army. The Science of Ordnance and Gunnery was constantly developing and each year marked an increase in firing accuracy, improvements in fire control, mine field effectiveness, ballistics or some other field of interest to the Coast Artillery. It was during this period that Fort Casey was at its finest, both in personnel and facilities. It was a time of relative elegance and power. It was a time of pride and esprit de corps, of discipline and patriotism. It was still a time of innocence. The soldiers of another war, serving at Casey, might lay claim to some of these virtues, but not all of them. When this "Golden Age" was over, it was lost forever and no amount of repainting or rebuilding could ever bring it back. World War I changed the world and Fort Casey as well.

Sadly, there are few left from those who served at Casey during this period. They are old with the years, but when disappearing guns, parade drill, and "The World War" are mentioned, their eyes still light up. Theirs was a time when large parts of the world were still a total mystery and war seemed, in some respects, still honorable. In early 1900, the light was just beginning to shine brightly on Coastal Defense and Fort Casey, and it would continue to do so until the "War to end all wars" forever changed the world. By 1918, Coastal Defense and Fort Casey entered into a new period and as one local resident observed, "It was a different world altogether inside the gates."[19]

CHAPTER FIVE

1918 - 1937: THE DECLINE BEGINS

Unprepared for the First World War, the Army instituted minor manpower increases in 1916, but these provided only enough men to guarantee the security of the nation's borders.[1] The Selective Service System created in 1917 would begin to remedy the manpower shortages almost immediately, as over nine million men would be registered for service in less than two months after Congress' War Declaration. The real problem now was what to do with these new recruits. How to adequately train and prepare these men for the battlefields of France in as short a time as possible would tax the military to its limits. The duty of the Coast Defense, as an essential branch of the Army, was twofold: the immediate defense of the nation's coasts and the training of hundreds of new soldiers in the use of artillery.

The coastal defense forts were perhaps somewhat better prepared than other branches of the U. S. military as the country entered the war. This is not to say, however, that Fort Casey and the other forts of Puget Sound were prepared for the flood of new troops or had kept up totally with the technological advances developed since 1914. The extravagant recommendations made by the Endicott Board in 1886 were never fully realized nor was the less ambitious project recommended by the Taft Board years later. What did result was an overlapping, two-stage fortification program that, by 1910, gave the United States a harbor defense system second to none in the world.[2]

Unfortunately for the Coast Artillery, technological developments coinciding with this same period were beginning to present a serious challenge to all existing harbor defenses, foreign as well as American. New techniques in fire-control and battleship turret designs now enabled some foreign ships to outrange, by a substantial margin, any harbor defense weapons within the United States. Onboard turrets could now elevate their guns to a much greater degree, which consequently sent the shells in a far higher arc of trajectory. Shells could now be directed not only at the armored sides of ships but also onto relatively horizontal surfaces such as decks. With these new higher firing angles, the open emplacements of the coastal defense now were extremely vulnerable as shells could be lobbed over the earth and protective concrete walls. Their openness was now a serious liability and the principal protective advantages developed for the disappearing carriage were now gone.

Equally important in this wartime period of advancement was the introduction of the airplane. The aviation age was in its infancy during World War I but the future prospects were making themselves more evident with each new day. During the war, the airplane was primarily used for observation or light bombing but there was also a desperate struggle for control of the skies. Opposing squadrons of fighters fought back and forth for air superiority. That control of air space was to mark a radical turning point in the effectiveness of American coastal fortifications. If an enemy were to control the air above the coastal defense forts, they could be rendered totally useless very quickly. The planes were slow and somewhat fragile, yet their potential for bringing destruction to open emplacements of any kind was obvious. By the time America entered the war in 1917, fortifications such as Fort Casey were fast becoming obsolete. The Coast Defense still had control of the waterways of Puget Sound. From the air, however, it was totally helpless.

Soon after America's entry into the war, it became clear that Germany would present no real danger of invasion. With this threat gone, it was decided to remove some of the smaller caliber guns from Fort Casey and the other forts of Admiralty Inlet. Less than a month after War was declared, suggestions were made to move the two 5-inch guns from Battery Turman to Willapa Bay on the coast and four of the eight 12-inch mortars from Battery Schenck to Deception Pass.³ This was not done immediately, but it illustrates how the integrity of the original fortifications now was threatened.

By September of 1917 work actually began on the removal of guns. Some were to be used aboard merchant ships; others were intended for shipment to France as much needed field artillery. For whatever reasons, the Corps of Engineers began dismounting the four 6-inch rifles of Battery Valleau in early October and the two 6-inch rifles of Battery Parker in late November. The gun tubes were removed, transported down to the Engineers Wharf and taken away by scow. The decline of Fort Casey had begun.⁴

In June, 1918, the #1 gun, (the only one left,) of Kingsbury, was removed, and was shipped out by scow as had the 6-inch batteries. The #2 gun was still resting on the ground within sight of its emplacement, but no mention was made of removing it. Finally, in May of 1919, an officer of the Coast Artillery on a routine inspection of the fort noted in his report to the Commanding General of the North Pacific Coast Artillery a need for the gun in Battery Kingsbury's number #2's emplacement. He determined, quite accurately, that emplacement number #2 was the only major caliber gun in any of the Admiralty Inlet forts that had the ability to fire at the inner harbor. It was the only one that could be used to fire at an enemy vessel that had sailed passed the triangle of destruction the forts created within Admiralty Inlet. This apparently caused concern, even though the war was over. Soon after the report was made, orders were issued that the gun was not to be salvaged but was to be remounted in emplacement #2. This was done in September of 1920. The soldiers were remounting gun #2 while the carriage from gun #1 was being cut up for scrap!⁵

Although the inadequacies of the coast artillery were becoming more apparent each day, plans were still being drawn up for changes and improvements in the existing forts. Though the United States did not have the time or the finances for the extensive modernization program needed at the forts, every effort was being made to make the existing fortifications as strong and well-defended as possible. In July of 1917, new range-finding equipment for the secondary batteries was installed, and in September, plans were drawn up for a new set of batteries at Partridge Point, a few miles north of Casey. These were to include two 16-inch rifles as well as mortars and rapid-fire support guns.

In June, 1918, the need for some form of protection from aerial attack received some attention; workers began the job of making the plotting rooms for the mortar batteries bomb proof. This concern for the airplane would continue, as definite plans were finally drawn up for antiaircraft gun emplacements. Following fairly closely the original recommendations made by Lieut. Col. Winslow in 1915, two batteries of two 3-inch fixed guns were to be installed. The first set was to be located at the north end of the reservation near the upper gate. The second battery was located in a field below and to the northeast of the mortars. The concern for completing these batteries seems to have lagged, as actual construction did not begin until June of 1920.⁶ The guns were placed completely out in the open, with no cover or camouflage of any type as per instructions. Planners decided a full 360 degree field of fire was more desirable than the potential safety of other gun batteries. The emplacements were located some distance from any other of the fort's emplacements; all ammunition and supplies had to be brought to the guns from other magazines. With no support structures built adjacent to the positions, electrical power was provided by large, portable storage batteries.

During the early months of the First World War, all available armament was manned at the forts

LEFT: Two soldiers in combat fatigues with their rifles and bayonets standing in front of one of the main barracks.

RIGHT: Baseball continued to be a big part of the local experience at Fort Casey before, during, and after the War. This view of the parade grounds from Officers' row shows a game in progress.

of the Puget Sound. In retrospect, the potential threat of a German invasion was very remote even in 1917, but this was not known by the soldiers of the Coastal Defense. The possibility of attack created just that much more tension and anxiety for the hundreds of new recruits manning the posts. There were 16 companies of Regular Army troops, the 1st through the 16th, and 12 companies of Washington National Guard, 17th through 28th, on duty in the Puget Sound District. In addition, at various times, 13 American Expeditionary Force (A.E.F.) Companies, 29th to 41st, were stationed in the area for last minute exercises before embarking for the European theatre.[7] All told, rosters of these early months list the names of 4,500 soldiers serving within the District. Throughout the War, manpower levels fluctuated, constantly dependent upon arrival of fresh troops and departure of men to other stations and to the European war zone.[8]

With the end of the war the United States seemed to be on the verge of making some sweeping changes in military preparedness. The government, shocked by the recent discoveries of its military weakness, appeared ready to support an army large enough and sufficiently well-armed to prevent a repetition of the un-preparedness of 1917.[9] Different support branches of the army were instructed to assemble and store such materials as to guarantee American military strength for some years to come. These orders however, were never fully carried out. In the first years immediately after the war there was a belief in the need for the maintaining of a sizeable military system. The armed services obviously believed this and so did many in the government. This belief was very soon swept away by a tide of public sentiment against anything military and with it went any hope of large appropriations. In Puget Sound, the end of the war saw the National Guard immediately begin to supplant regular army troops at the forts. The regulars at Admiralty Head were moved into tents behind the main batteries, then slowly transferred to new posts for discharge. Troop strength steadily declined at all the forts of the Sound. This was a reflection of falling manpower levels throughout the nation. Troop levels fell from 3,710,463 as of November 11, 1918 to 264,500 by the beginning of 1920. In the Puget Sound District, the strength of gun batteries in the harbor defense network dropped from its high of 4,500 men of all ranks to 50 officers and 884 enlisted men by March, 1919.[10]

Armament also was down. Guns from all the forts had been siphoned away. In May, 1918, the two 5-inch rapid-fire rifles of Battery Turman were removed and shipped to Sandy Hook, New Jersey. Also removed were the two forward mortars in each of the two pits of Battery Seymour. These were sent to an Engineering Plant in Ohio. By 1919, 13 guns of various calibers had been removed from Fort Casey and the total for the forts of Admiralty Inlet was down from 102 guns to 66.[11]

This did not, however, stop construction or experimental projects that had been started during or immediately after the war. They were slowed considerably, but this depended on their percentage of completion at war's end. At Fort Casey, a new communications switchboard was turned over by the Signal Corps to the Coast Artillery in October 1919. This new reinforced concrete building was located across from Battery Trevor and was built into a hillside for added protection. In 1920 work was also begun on the 3-inch antiaircraft batteries. This project, however, got caught up in the post-war withdrawal of military funds and took until late 1922 to finish just the four emplacements. The guns themselves were not mounted until early 1923, and the battery was not completed until May of that year.[12]

A series of experiments took place soon after the war, dealing with fire-control and lighter-than-air craft. The experimentation was an attempt to improve the firing accuracy of the fixed coast artillery. Gunnery experts of the day believed that land-based observation stations used for fixed guns had reached the limit of their efficiency. The range of the weapons now in use was dramatically increasing and causing problems with accuracy. The probability of error resulting from these long ranges which were required during the War was a serious concern and would again become a problem in future conflicts.[13] Partly as a test of a new service that had been developing during the war and partly because of appropriation cutbacks that prevented installation of heavier caliber weapons at the forts of Admiralty Inlet, the testing of lighter-than-air craft was authorized. The trials called for spotting targets from balloons as means of increasing firing accuracy. It was hoped that by using lighter-than-air craft at the end of a baseline, it would be possible to actually direct fire on moving targets and improve on the limits reached by land based observation stations.

Balloons as observation platforms for fire-control had played a limited yet effective role during the First World War, and now the Ordnance branch of the Army ordered further study. The Air Service Officers in the Lighter-than-air Branch had planned in early 1919 to begin tests but were unable to officially begin until 1920. Experiments were conducted in Puget Sound and San Francisco. On May 11, 1920, the first detachment of officers and enlisted men arrived at Fort Worden and on May 16th, the men of the 2nd Balloon Company were ferried to Casey. Tests were conducted with sausage or observation balloons and spherical or free balloons. Each Company was equipped with one of each type. The sausage-type balloons had baskets attached to their underside, in which the spotters were to ride. Each company was to work closely with the Artillery to develop the complete cooperation needed to make aerial fire-control practical.

During May, tests were conducted with the helium-filled balloons in establishing base firing lines, observation over water of long range targets, photographing terrain surrounding the forts, measuring atmospheric conditions at heights of 2,000 feet, and even parachute jumps.[14] Improved fire-control, however, was the main goal. Once the balloons were filled, they were allowed to rise, with a heavy cable attached. When the day's work was completed the balloon was brought down by a ratchet-type crank or at times by employing a team of mules to pull in the cable. The major disadvantage and real limiting factor in using the balloons was the condition of the winds while flying. On a number of occasions high winds cancelled flights or made it impossible to get accurate observations.[15] Still, these experiments proved satisfactory enough to warrant the upgrading of the Balloon Companies to the strength of Coast Artillery. Based on the recommendations of the military observers present during the experiments, it was decided to build two balloon hangers. One was constructed at Fort Worden and the other at Casey. Contracts were awarded for the construction of the two units, each at a cost of $85,000.[16]

The Admiralty Head hangar was located in a field to the northeast of the parade grounds in what one soldier at the fort described as the best wheat growing land on the post. The group of four buildings for the Balloon Service consisted of a steel hanger, a generator house, a storehouse, and a garage. The hanger was constructed of steel covered with galvanized iron, 120 by 76 feet that rose to an elevation of 60 feet. The generator house was of steel construction based on a concrete foundation, 80 feet square. The frame storehouse was 30 by 70 feet, and the frame garage 30 by 60 feet.[17] Six acres of land were cleared for the construction of the buildings and the safe operation of the balloons. There

ABOVE: The Balloon Hanger soon after completion in 1921. A somewhat ill-advised program that was doomed to failure seemingly before the paint was dry on the structure. Local residents spoke of more than one of the gas filled balloons breaking free and heading for Bremerton. Unlike its duplicate at Fort Worden, the Casey Hanger was allowed to deteriorate and would be removed by 1939. The Fort Worden hanger is still in use today.

LEFT: One of the 2 original Anti-aircraft gun batteries installed at Casey in 1921. This emplacement was located near the upper gate and like its partner was completely out in the open. The base security by this time was not the best as this local civilian and his daughter were able to walk up to the gun and have their picture taken. Note the Balloon Hanger in the background.

RIGHT: The entrance to the new Switchboard which was turned over to the Fort in 1919. This was one of the first attempts to provide protection from the new developments in high angle artillery and possible aerial assault.

were some construction delays, especially with the huge hangar. The contractor had a difficult time getting structural steel as it was still in short supply from the War. Because of these delays the hangar was not finished until August 17, 1921.

Ironically, very soon after the completion of the Balloon Hangar, the Lighter-than-air branch of the air service was withdrawn from the Puget Sound and transferred to San Francisco. The attempts to set up base end observation positions, one at Casey and one at Worden, to direct fire just did not work out. After a promising beginning and the construction of the hanger facilities at both forts, the Ordnance Department had a change of heart. With the completion of the hangers and their support structures, the Balloon Service resumed testing. Apparently, the results just did not meet the desired expectations. The degree of accuracy necessary could never be achieved because of the wind conditions in Admiralty Inlet. Observers were unable to keep their telescopes on the objectives at all times because of the constantly shifting winds. The Air Service detachment was transferred to Fort Lewis, Washington, and for the next few years the hanger was used for storage and as a shelter for the post cattle. Some local residents even recalled playing tennis on the large cement floor. As years passed and Fort Casey drifted into caretaker status, the building was not maintained and slowly deteriorated in the salt air. The rusting structure was removed sometime between 1938 and 1939.[18]

Congress, meanwhile, had begun examining limitations on the Army and its defensive military structure. The War Department made recommendations on standards for national troop strength and funding, but the National Defense Act of 1920 set manpower levels lower than the military had suggested, and even these were not reached, as Congress failed to appropriate sufficient funds for support. For at least the next 15 years, support for the Army and Coastal Defense could be characterized by a lack of funds, shortages of personnel, and public indifference. This hampered all operations at the forts of the Coastal Defense in the years after the war. Economy of operation became the watchword of Army appropriations. This was to become much more than just belt tightening. As the nation moved into the prolonged economic depression that followed the stock market crash in 1929, it became almost strangulation. In the midst of the ensuing retrenchment, the Secretary of War noted the successive reductions in military appropriations had been absorbed by

"Continuing in service obsolete and inefficient equipment, and where absolutely necessary, by suspending technical research and development work."[19]

The condition of Fort Casey during the 1920's mirrored the state of military appropriations for coastal defense. There was to be a slow but steady reduction in personnel and in the facility itself. As the size of the Army decreased, so did the support branches. The Quartermaster Corps, which had been responsible for the construction of all the permanent barracks, quarters, shops, storehouses and other miscellaneous buildings for the troops at Fort Casey, was cut back to the extent that it could no longer properly maintain these structures. The Corps of Engineers was able to maintain supervisory personnel at the fort, but only until the latter part of 1924. From then on all the forts of the Inlet were under the direction of a single director stationed at Fort Worden. Maintenance of the artillery emplacements became the sole duty of the soldiers based at the fort and as their numbers fell so did the level of service and repair. The drastic cut backs in funding all but eliminated money to repair equipment and funds to hire civilian employees. Many of the buildings that had been built to house and service the large numbers of men stationed at Fort Casey were allowed to deteriorate or were torn down and burned.

The attitude of the men stationed at Fort Casey was also affected. It was obvious to them that the Coast Defense was moving into a period of austerity and their demeanor reflected this. The garrison became the stopping off place for retiring officers and misfits from other posts. The pay for the soldiers was reduced and the camp was showing signs of wear and neglect. The men became very disillusioned, and indifference supplanted the efficiency that had been present only a few years earlier.[20]

There were a few bright spots during the early part of the 1920s that kept garrison duty from becoming totally routine, but they were few. General John J. Pershing visited the area in January 1920, stopping only to briefly inspect Fort Worden. The men at Casey could only wonder about "Black Jack" as his steamer *Kitsap II* sailed up the Inlet to Seattle. A general who did visit the fort in 1920 found much to be concerned about. Major General Frank W. Coe, on an inspection as Chief of Coast Artillery, concluded that most of the guns were useless against the modern battleships now sailing the oceans. Following his visit, all the empty carriages from dismounted guns were removed. Batteries Valleau, Parker, Turman, gun position #1 of Kingsbury, and the forward two carriages in each pit of Seymour were scrapped. The gun wells were either filled with sand and cemented or covered over with planking. Some 2,000 tons of gun carriages from Forts Casey and Worden were cut up and hauled to Seattle for sale as scrap metal.[21]

There was a brief influx of new men in March of 1920 when the War Department authorized small increases in the Washington National Guard. Many of the men were from tours of service in the Philippines or other locations. It was hoped that by the end of the year all three of the Admiralty Inlet forts would reach the full strength for which they were authorized. This was not to be. Training continued at all of the forts, with practice firing of the big guns still carried out on a regular basis. Corps of Engineer records indicate a target practice session for Battery Worth took place on May 31, 1923. The target, towed by the mine planter *Ringgold*, was destroyed with the 11th shot.[22]

An unusual incident took place in Admiralty Inlet on the morning of July 27, 1923. President Warren G. Harding, traveling on board the transport ship *Henderson*, was on his way from Vancouver to Seattle. He was to visit both Vancouver and Seattle to give speeches while enroute to San Francisco. After leaving Vancouver on the morning of the 27th, the Henderson's escort squadron encountered a heavy fog that had blanketed Vancouver Harbor and Puget Sound. Visibility was reported down to less than 50 yards; captains were having great difficulty identifying the numerous fog whistles that were constantly sounding as the convoy sailed into Admiralty Inlet. A number of ships lost sight of each other. Suddenly, the escorting destroyer *Zeilen* sighted the *Henderson* off the port quarter on a course converging with her own. At 7:56 am, the huge transport struck the *Zeilen* amidships. There was a grinding crash, then the cry of "All hands on deck!"[23]

The collision was described as slight on board the *Henderson* and the President's ship continued on its way to Seattle. The destroyer *Zeilen*, however, was not so lucky. The transport had punched a rather large hole in its side. The amount of water coming in, even in the relatively calm waters of Admiralty Inlet, was causing a considerable list to port. Matters were complicated aboard the *Zeilen* because the collision had severed the ship's main steam lines, which supplied power to all the ship's

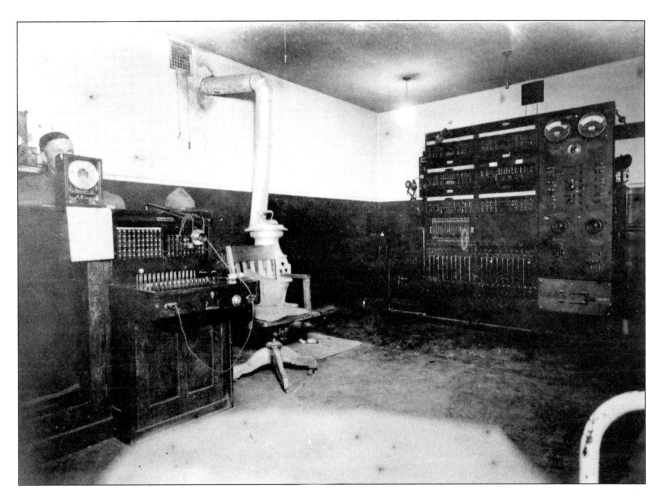

ABOVE: Inside the Switchboard at Fort Casey. All communication for the entire fort passed through this communication center. The switchboard is on the left and the power controls are on the right.

LEFT: By the late 1920's Fort Casey was designated as a fortification in caretaker status. Breech blocks were removed and stored against the weather, railings and walkways were removed, and the emplacements, for the most part, received little maintenance. The lack of care is visible both on the 10" disappearing rifle and the concrete parapet.

pumps. Despite securing all water-tight compartments, the list increased. Twenty-eight minutes after the impact, the *Zeilen's* list was at 35 degrees. It appeared the ship would roll over and sink. When the destroyer continued to take on water and the list reached 40 degrees, Captain James Forance gave orders to abandon ship.

While crewmen were being picked up by other ships in the convoy, the *USS Nicholas* and the *USS Corry*, the Captain and a small group of men stood off the destroyer in a small boat to await the final outcome. When after ten minutes the list hadn't increased the Captain and his small band of men returned and attached a tow line from the *Nicholas*. The *Zeilen* was towed toward Admiralty Head where it was hoped the anchor could be dropped to hold the ship until tugs arrived. Unfortunately the strong ebb tide caused the anchor to drag and the ship continued to drift.[24]

By this time, soldiers at Fort Casey had been alerted to the drama taking place in the waters in front of the main gun emplacements and they attempted to lend a hand. An alert sergeant and a hastily gathered group of men managed to secure a line from the *Zeilen*. Using a steam-powered tractor, they tried to pull the stricken ship closer to shore and to better anchor the cable. The swift ebb tide and the size of the ship, however, proved to be too much for the small steam donkey. All they apparently were able to do was to slow down the ship's drift. Fortunately, an Army tug soon arrived on the scene and the still listing *Zeilen* was pulled into the Engineer's dock at Casey. There, it was pumped out so that the damage could be better assessed. The *Zeilen* eventually limped into Bremerton for repairs, but not before a pair of enterprising young Coupeville brothers had taken a horse-and-buggy load of apples down to the dock to sell to the sailors on board.

Mickey Clark, the younger member of the apple salesmen and a lifelong resident of Coupeville, remembered doing this sort thing quite often with the soldiers at the post.

> *The original barracks were built in a large 'U' shape with a circular cement walk inside the 'U'. Wagons could drive up behind the barracks to deliver goods. Each barrack had its own kitchen facing this drive up where the cooks would be at work preparing meals. My brother and I would pick apples, plums, and cherries to sell to the soldiers. We would sell a 5 pound lard bucket full to the soldiers for 10¢. Everyone thought they were getting a deal. The soldiers would fill their campaign hats full and walk away eating the fresh fruit.*[25]

Though Fort Casey and the Coast Artillery were in a steady decline, this friendly spirit and somewhat relaxed military atmosphere prevailed. Local newspapers still announced regular Y.M.C.A. gatherings and activities for the soldiers and local residents. Entertaining the men with music and homemade delights was just one of the ways the fort's neighbors expressed their appreciation to the troops and the job they were doing. Baseball continued to be a real rallying force as large numbers of spectators regularly showed up for big games the Casey team played against the other forts or nearby towns. It was one of the few extracurricular activities for the men stationed on "The Rock."

In late 1924, the old workers' bunkhouse and cookhouse, built on the Crockett's Lake spit, were sold and removed. The buildings had been constructed in the early days of the fort but had been unused for some time because of appropriations cutbacks. An event of somewhat more significance that took place in 1924 was the formation of the 14th Coast Artillery Regiment. Created by the

ABOVE: By the late 1930's Fort Casey was close to abandonment. These pictures of the main barracks being demolished in 1937 by a private contractor were just another example of the neglect the fort had been subjected too during the past 10 years. These barracks had the capacity to house over 100 men with their own kitchen and dining hall. Similar structures are still standing and being used at Fort Worden today.

War Department, it was a measure to streamline the organization of the coast artillery in the Puget Sound District. The twelve designated companies were disbanded and all personnel transferred to new batteries, listed in alphabetical order from A to K, minus J. At the time of its organization, July 1, 1924, the regiment comprised 21 officers and 400 enlisted men.[26]

This put the defense of Puget Sound in a further reduced state, for this limited number of men were to occupy the five forts of the harbor defense. The vast majority of these men were stationed at Fort Worden, the headquarters of the Coast Defense in the Puget Sound since 1903. These soldiers were garrison troops. Training was to continue in a limited fashion, the buildings and emplacements were to be maintained as much as funds would allow, and the forts remained as token guardians of Puget Sound.

Manpower levels of the 14th Coast Artillery fluctuated from year to year throughout the 1920s and 1930s. The low point was hit in October 1926, when the level fell to 300 enlisted men and just 19 officers.[27] This was just a further reflection of the national mood. The belief continued that we would not be involved in any future wars. Despite warnings of Japan's economic ambitions in the Pacific after World War I and the writings of men like Alfred Thayer Mahan and Billy Mitchell, the country and the government publicly continued to believe war was a thing of the past.

Speeches given in Congress during the 66th (1919-1921) and 69th (1925-1927) secessions point to this belief. Coast defense was no longer vital to the protection of our nation if there was no threat. The war to end all wars had made the world safe for democracy, hadn't it? Missouri Senator James A. Reed asked: "Who are we going to fight?" Congressman William A. Ayres of Kansas stated: "There is no evidence of this country being attacked by any other nation in the near future." Congressman Charles R. Evans of Nevada insisted: "Never in history was military training so little needed.[28] Despite the dark clouds that were beginning to form in Asia and Europe, all seemed right in the world.

The strain on under strength detachments at all of the forts eased somewhat in July, 1927. What had been in practice for some time now became formally acknowledged. The Secretary of War, in a letter sent to the Commanding General of the Army, made it clear that certain forts and harbor defenses across the country were now in a caretaking status because of the reduced strength of the Coast Artillery. The Secretary was quick to point out that the fortifications were not being abandoned and were to be maintained in such conditions as to insure full operation without delay in case of threatened emergency. The message was dated July 13, 1927.[29] Forts Flagler, Whitman, Ward, and Casey were placed on a caretaking basis.

The number of troops at Fort Casey was steadily reduced. In 1926 records list a camp population of 90 men. By the end of 1927, the number was down to four officers and 45 enlisted men. The numbers kept dropping until there was a mere handful under the command of Master Sergeant, William Nelson. The fort was to remain in the charge of this small group until late in the 1930s. With less than a full platoon at the fort, the repair and maintenance work carried out on a fortification complex covering over 500 acres could only be of a limited nature. Corps of Engineer records show the work mostly dealt with painting and weatherizing. The men patched cracks in concrete, fixed leaking roofs, replaced broken windows, and made constant checks on magazine dryness and the conditions of armament. The guns were periodically moved on their bases to prevent damage to the concrete emplacements. The heavy carriages were rotated and the guns elevated up and down to forestall settling. To prevent the guns from rusting, they were liberally coated in Cosmoline. This jellylike substance was well known in the army as a preservative and was spread all over the guns and their carriages to protect them from the salt water.

The men in charge of caretaking at Casey and their families were free to live in any of the quarters on the nearly deserted reservation. The children had the run of the fort. Billie Smith, daughter of Sergeant Nelson, who was in charge of the fort from the mid 1920s until the late 1930's, remembered playing on the reservation:

> *We could go just about anywhere we wanted. We would go into the big emplacements, sliding down the angled concrete walls, climbing on the guns, down on the beach, running and screaming in the dark tunnels, and even to the top of the lighthouse. It was our playground.*"[30]

The Corps of Engineers kept a more direct contact with the maintenance of their portion of the fort. Though restricted by money and manpower, the Corps was able to maintain an Assistant Engineer at the fort during the 1930s. There were monthly inspections from the District Engineer stationed at Worden, and for the most part, the gun emplacements and their support structures were properly cared for. This was not the case with the Quartermaster Corps. Their cutbacks all but eliminated any but the most cursory care for the various buildings and living quarters. The three large permanent barracks that were built in 1904, in particular, were allowed to deteriorate. Their portion of the fort was allowed to sit and weather. It may seem strange to use the phrase, "their portion of the fort" but it must be remembered that, while all were part of the same Army, the different branches (Engineers, Quartermaster, Signal, Ordnance) were not on the best of terms. Each had its own commanding officer, its own budget, and its own responsibilities. Coordination between branches might be close during wartime; in peacetime, it was tenuous at best. Even back in 1900, there were separate docks built at the fort, one for Engineers and one for the Quartermaster.

The early 1930s, for the most part, saw the condition of Coastal Defense, like the Army in general, go from bad to worse. The Great Depression and the continuing antiwar sentiment in the country made the whole question of military appropriations a touchy issue. The national mood was hostile to any measure which might expand the Army. The hope of maintaining a strong military force in early 1920 had descended into unbelievable levels of stagnation.

The Army during the 1920s and early 30s may have been less ready to function as a fighting force than at any time in history. It lacked even the combat capacity that the campaigns had forced on it during the nineteenth century.[31] Writing his war memoirs about this time, General Peyton C. March, Army Chief of Staff after World War I, commented that the United States, on its own initiative, had rendered itself more impotent than Germany under the military limitations of the Treaty of Versailles.[32]

In August of 1933, there was a brief increase of activity. The Signal Corps installed a new radio installation at Casey. The old Switchboard house, which had been sitting empty since the construction of the reinforced concrete Switchboard in 1919, was converted by August and two radio masts erected close by. The Corps of Engineers constructed the eight foot masts and helped in building conversion.[33]

By 1936, Fort Casey was approaching abandonment. Its days of usefulness seemed long past. The remaining, now ancient guns, no longer were fired; the men who once had taken such pride in their gunnery skills and esprit de corps were in their 40s. The period of time from 1918 to 1937 was a sad time for the Coastal Defense. What had once been modern and great was now old and weathered. Alfalfa now grew on the parade ground, and the sentry posts sat abandoned and empty. The main barracks had become unusable from lack of attention. The roads of the post were pock-marked with holes. The Engineer's dock and its approach had fallen to pieces and were beyond repair.

Fort Casey had become relatively useless as a coastal defense fortification. Developments in the science of warfare made fixed coastal batteries as designed at the turn of the century obsolete. Ships could shoot further than the fort's guns and the airplane had come along. With evolution of aviation the forts lost all the protection the thick parapets and ingenious carriages had once provided. As one old sergeant remarked, *"In 1927, when three planes landed on the vacant parade grounds at Casey, I could see the complete uselessness of the fort."*[34]

CHAPTER SIX

WORLD WAR II

D URING 1936, THE ARMY GENERAL STAFF CONDUCTED A COMPLETE REVIEW OF ITS WAR MOBILIZATION plan. Trying to be as honest as possible concerning what the Army of 1936 was actually capable of accomplishing in the event of war, the planners came to the conclusion that the only troops they could count on early in an emergency mobilization were the 110,000 of the Regular Army. The military estimated that they could feed, clothe, transport, and shelter those troops which would be mustered during the first thirty days, from equipment on hand. They could not, however, properly supply such things as airplanes, tanks, combat cars, scout cars, antiaircraft guns, .50 caliber machine guns, and possibly organizational motor equipment. They also noted that there would be shortages in gas masks, radio and telephone equipment and medical supplies.[1]

This, then, was the sorry state of the United States Army in 1936. The encouraging possibilities the passage of the National Defense Act of 1920 had raised for maintaining a strong National Army had been lost during the 1920s and early 1930s. The gloom of the Depression and years of curtailed expenditures of money had left the Army as nothing more than a small school for soldiers, relying upon worn and obsolete equipment. There were some military leaders, however, who desperately fought this stagnation of the military. They accurately saw the potential danger to a nation that could not adequately protect itself. One, in particular, who was to have a dramatic, far reaching influence on the Army of the 1940s, was Army Chief of Staff, Malin Craig. As head of the Army, he relentlessly pursued realistic planning and preparedness.[2] Craig perceptively saw that, in an uncertain world, the Army could not depend upon mobilization plans requiring years to be realized. The Army had to be as ready as possible to fight.

By the end of 1936 and throughout 1937, Congressional support for Malin Craig's ideas began to stir. Events in Europe and the Far East were making Congress and the President much more receptive to improving the Armed Forces. A rebuilding program for the Navy had been initiated as early as 1934 and increases for military appropriations were approved by Congress in 1938. Unfortunately, the movement to rearm was still very slow and, in many ways, woefully inadequate. The status of the Army and Coastal Defense continued in the depressed state it had been since the early 1930s.

Events in Europe and the orient during 1938, however, pushed the president to make new, revised requests to speed up his rearmament program. Germany's annexation of Austria and the humiliation of Czechoslovakia moved Roosevelt to offer a new plan in November. The president wanted to send enough support to European democracies that it would cause Germany and Italy to pause in their ambitions. America could then stay neutral. By September of 1939, all of these hopes would be gone, as would the integrity of Poland's borders.

At Admiralty Head, life continued much as it had since the late 1920s. Fort Casey, along with Forts Ward, Flagler, and Whitman, had been under caretaker status since 1928. At each post, a small detachment of Coast Artillery personnel had been stationed. Their job was to guard government property, but also to carry out orders issued in 1927 by the Secretary of War to maintain the forts and "to keep them in condition for a prompt restoration to an active system."[3] Unfortunately, these orders took money to carry out and appropriations for maintenance and repairs were continually short of what was actually needed. In 1935, for example, maintenance appropriations for all Army establishments in the United States were $1,670,364. This was only 61% of what was needed to meet the minimum estimated requirements of Army installations. In effect, this meant that the small, older posts, particular those of Coastal Defense in outlying areas, got very little attention. Less than a year after the Secretary of War's orders concerning maintenance were issued, there were already signs of neglect and wear at Casey. Reports from May 16, 1928, list the buildings as still "ok" but notes that the roads of the post were full of potholes and the Engineers' dock had fallen to pieces. The Corps of Engineers' Inspector who made the report estimated the roads could be repaired for $4,500. The repair budget designated to Casey for the year was listed at $542.26.[4]

As 1937 began, interest increased in the forts of Puget Sound. Although the forts were still in caretaker status, Engineer reports showed a marked increase in work projects. The small detachment of men began to spend much more time on weatherizing and waterproofing. The magazines, which were being used to store ammunition for those guns still mounted, were of prime importance, as was electrical wiring that was being repaired or replaced around the post. In March, the concern over air defense led to a work project for new antiaircraft batteries below the mortars. The work, however, went extremely slow due to the bare trickle of funds that were released from the District Headquarters, and the three gun emplacement would not be completed for over a year. Continual requests for supplementary equipment that was essential for the proper operation of the antiaircraft batteries came back month after month marked "No money available."

While the increased maintenance work showed a renewed interest, the fort itself was still in sad condition. The three main enlisted men's barracks, built in 1905, had deteriorated to a state beyond repair, and along with a number of the post auxiliary buildings, would have to be torn down. During 1938-39, eighteen buildings were salvaged on the post. The experimental balloon hangar that had been rusting away since 1924 was removed as were the original cantonment barracks built at the turn of the century. Many of these buildings could have been preserved if they had been cared for properly. Structures of identical design and construction were still in use at Fort Worden. The submarine fire-control cables between the three forts of Admiralty Inlet had been broken in the early 1930s and had never been repaired. Fort Casey could contact Fort Flagler for target information but not the Harbor Defense Headquarters at Fort Worden. The guns that were still mounted at Casey were listed as being in a "C" classification of readiness, meaning they could be brought into service in 72 hours. In all probability, this was only true on paper. The 10-inch guns of Batteries of Worth, Moore, and Kingsbury had been totally inactive for a number of years and were completely coated in Cosmoline for weatherization. The other guns of Batteries Seymour, Schenck, and Van Horne had been used in National Guard training at times, but were basically in the same condition as the other guns. The fort still was under the command of a single Master Sergeant and garrisoned by less than 45 troops.[5]

Despite orders to keep forts like Casey in a "caretaker" not "abandonment" status condition at Admiralty Head continued to deteriorated. The true lack of attention was embarrassingly shown to the local military when on March 6, 1938, two men were arrested by F.B.I. agents for stealing lead from the counterweights of the 10-inch batteries to sell as scrap metal. Newspaper reports, which tended to exaggerate some of the details, claimed the two men had removed some 16,000 pounds of lead over a period of weeks.[6] Had there been sufficient troops at the post to keep the guns in a 72 hour readiness state, this removal of lead from the counterweight wells would have been noticed. Yet the two men removed eight tons of metal from a military post at night without being detected

Events during 1939 continued to push the President and the nation toward rearmament. Congress

ABOVE: A detachment of Battery A, 14th Coast Artillery, standing in front of their barracks at Fort Worden in 1939. These men were some of the first to be transferred to Fort Casey to begin the reconditioning of the heavy guns and bringing the fort back to life. Sergeant Roy Engom is second from the left in the second row.

RIGHT: Menu for Christmas Dinner at Fort Casey for the 14th Coast Artillery, Battery "A". Sergeant's Roy Engom and Don Lee were present.

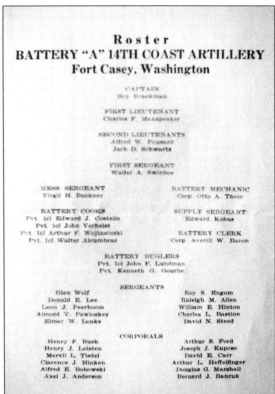

ABOVE: A Christmas Dinner that must have been somewhat somber after the events at Pearl Harbor only 18 days earlier. The initial shock had worn off but the threat of invasion was still present.

BELOW: 12-inch railway mounted mortars, like these near Fort Stevens at the mouth of the Columbia River, were positioned at various places along the Washington Coast in the early months of the war until the basic defenses of the Northwest were brought up to a ready state.

passed a Supplementary Appropriations Act which lifted the ceiling on monthly enlistment strength and provided funds to enlarge the air and ground forces of the nation and equip them with the latest weapons. Also authorized was the first major military construction program since 1918. Between January 1939 and March 1940, approximately $175 million became available for building purposes. This was still a small amount in comparison with the mobilization and war efforts that were to follow, but the Expansion Program, nevertheless, was "a real start... toward placing the Army on a bases of preparedness."[7]

By the summer of 1939 the nation's military forces had improved to a level in which they were somewhat stronger than they had been during the early 1930s. The Navy was by far best-prepared for the coming struggle, while the Army and the Coast Defense were still, for the most part, preparing for a war in the styles of 1918. The total strength of the Regular Army, officers and men, was approaching 190,000 but they were scattered all over the nation and throughout the outlying possessions. The 140,000 within the United States were still scattered (in a fashion remarkably reminiscent of the days of the Indian Wars) among 130 posts chiefly of battalion size.[8] Though the Army was stronger and better prepared for action than it was in the early 1930s, it was still numerically far weaker than the army of any other world power. There was not a single division among its continental forces ready for immediate action.[9]

The Coast Defense in Puget Sound was in even worse condition. Except for Fort Worden, which had remained in active service throughout the 1920s and 1930s, all of the posts were in poor repair, completely undermanned and, for the most part, still using World War I or earlier equipment. The soldiers at Fort Casey, like all others in the Army, were still using the 1903 model Springfield rifle, and the .50-caliber machine gun was the basic anti-tank weapon. The newest pieces of artillery within the Puget Sound Harbor defense, larger than 3-inch, were 1903 vintage and none of the guns at any of the forts had any protection from aerial attack. At Casey and Flagler, in particular, the barracks which would be desperately needed to house the flood of new troops the war would bring, were beyond saving. Years of neglect left them only fit for salvage. Fort Casey was beginning its second world war in tattered clothes, armed with outdated weapons.

In one important respect, however, the Army, and therefore Coastal Defense, was further ahead in 1939 than ever before in peacetime - planning for its own future.[10] The National Defense Act of 1920 had gone a long way toward setting a better foundation for a permanent military policy than the United States had ever had. The strengthening of the General Staff of the Army during and after World War I and the realistic planning which Malin Craig had insisted upon since 1936 had given the Army a capacity for direct growth. This unhindered ability to grow and expand when the need arose allowed plans to be created in weeks rather than months or years. Considering how unstable and confused the world situation was becoming and with an undefined national direction this flexibility for growth would be the Army's real strength in the coming months. The framework for planning and command had been built in and improved upon since 1920 and now would meet the test of a second world war.

During the period of time from the European declarations of war on September 3, 1939, and Americas' entry, the nation prepared for war in a more organized and purposeful way than in 1914-17.[11] There was better preparation, although much more could have been accomplished had it not been for the still vocal anti-involvement sentiment in the nation and the President's cautious concern for it. In September, when war had been declared in Europe, the President declared a "limited national emergency." He allowed increases in Regular Army and National Guard recruitment but still not to the 280,000 levels authorized by the National Defense Act of 1920. He submitted a new Army Budget of $853 million in early 1940. This was still far below what the General Staff, now under the direction of George C. Marshall, estimated in terms of the possible needs of war. Marshall defended the amount by saying, *"If Europe blazed in the late spring or early summer, we must put our house in order before the sparks reach the Western Hemisphere."*[12]

Before the Senate could act on Roosevelt's appropriations, Europe did indeed blaze. In the next few months the shock of the French collapse and the swiftness of the German blitzkrieg sent ripples throughout America. Fears that both the British and French fleets might fall into German hands and the now very real threat to the Western Hemisphere forced aside the monetary caution of Congress. The Senate Appropriations Committee now urged the president to submit new defense estimates, and both the Senate and the House were quick to support Roosevelt's supplemental appropriations request of $732 million. Hearings were held on Marshall's appeals for raising manpower levels in the Army.

All of this was taking place against the backdrop of the 1940 presidential elections and continued resistance by isolationists in and out of Congress. This politically powerful group fought hard to keep the arms embargo, to prevent Roosevelt from implementing Lend-Lease in 1941 and, above all, to keep America out of war. This was by no means a small or isolated movement. The public debate over the relative merits of isolationism and intervention was to be found in all parts of the country and could trace its roots back to the 1930s. Roosevelt, ever conscious of public opinion, tried to stay in the middle of the road. Though he was accused of engaging in self-delusion, the President's policy of hoping for the best while preparing for the worst expressed the predominant sense of the American people in 1940.[13]

The movement to rearm and prepare for the possibilities of war began to take effect in Puget Sound in the latter part of 1940. The Commanding officer of Fort Worden, Colonel James H. Cunningham, was placed in charge of organizing a modernization program for the Coast Defense. This program began in September, 1940, and would continue well into 1943. The initial project, drafted by Cunningham's staff, called for the installation of three 16-inch and four 6-inch gun batteries with the accompanying base-end stations, searchlights, radar, and other accessories. The plan was to establish a line of defense from Cape Flattery, on the Olympic Peninsula to Deception Pass, covering some 125 miles. The modernization program also called for the remaining of the forts of the Harbor Defense that had been idle for so long. Fort Casey, along with Forts Flagler, Whitman and Ward were given new life and would again be part of the defensive framework of the nation.[14]

The first troops to arrive at Admiralty Head came in late September, 1940. Twenty-two "Master Gunners," as they were called, of the 14th Coast Artillery, Battery A, were transferred from Fort Worden. Upon their arrival, they found the post was still under the command of Master Sergeant Nelson and the living accommodations scarce. Since the main barracks had been razed in 1937, along with a number of the officers quarters, the men, all 22 of them, were billeted in the Colonel's quarters. One of the "Master Gunners" to arrive in September was Private Don Lee. Concerning the housing he commented, *"With all of us staying in the one house it was pretty crowded. There were three of us bunking up in the peak of the house. It was really tough to get all the way up there on those late Saturday nights!"*[15]

The first assignment of these new arrivals was to recondition all the heavy guns still at the fort; this included the 10-inch disappearing rifles at Moore, Worth, and Kingsbury, the 12-inch mortars at Seymour and Schenck, and the 3-inch rapid fire at Van Horne and Trevor. Batteries Valleau, Parker, and Turman were empty. The reconditioning meant removing the protective Cosmoline that had been liberally spread over all parts of the guns and carriages. Up to 1/2 inch of this heavy, jelly like substance was everywhere, particularly the barrel, inside and out, to try and protect the guns from rust. These weapons were all close to 40 years old and other than the cosmoline and removing the breech blocks for inside storage, had no other coverings or protections from the weather and salt air. Once the guns were cleaned they then had to be oiled, greased and any broken parts replaced. The guns were finally test-fired with full caliber ammunition, in most cases, for the first time in almost 15 years.

In January, 1941, a total review of Harbor Defenses in the Puget Sound was carried out as a part of the Modernization Program. All the Coastal Defense forts were inspected, inventoried, and recommendations made for future use. At Fort Casey the report covered weapons, fire control, searchlights, base protection and gas protection. The only weapons considered still usable were the 3-inch guns of Battery Van Horne and the 12-inch mortars of Batteries Seymour and Schenck. The 10-inch guns were not considered practical or protected enough for the men to operate. The mobile antiaircraft guns were totally out in the open. Fire control for these guns was provided by 9 and 15-foot coincidence range finders and depression positions finders (DPF's) located at the Fort and in the area. Only four of the five original fixed searchlights were still usable. The fifth light had to be removed because of deterioration.[16]

It was recommended that the base add further protection for its batteries and the beach areas facing Admiralty Inlet by installing double gun .50 caliber antiaircraft weapons stations. Additional fire support would come from six platoons of 24-.30 caliber machine guns. Since there was no protection for gas attacks, efforts would be made to gas-proof all permanent structures.[17]

Along with the Modernization Program, an Anti-Motor Torpedo Boat (AMTB) Defense was also begun in 1941. Certain guns were resited so as to serve both Antiaircraft (AA) and AMTB functions. To meet this new AMTB need, 90mm and 37mm fixed and mobile guns were established at various locations around the area. Two mobile 90mm's were put at Deception Pass, two fixed 37mm guns were placed along Saratoga Passage near Fort Whitman, two fixed 90mm guns were put at Ebey's Landing, and two mobile 90mm guns were stationed at Admiralty Head. All told there were 20 AMTB gun positions within the Puget Sound Harbor Defense command.[18]

An under-water defense system was also formally established in 1941. Originally begun as an experimental hydrophone project in 1937, two permanent positions were eventually in operation by 1942. One was located on Marrowstone Island, near Fort Flagler; the other was built at Greenbank, near the southern end of the Casey reservation. These hydrophone stations, along with experimental magnetic loops installed at the entrance to Admiralty Inlet in July, 1942, operated as an early warning detection system for submarines and surface vessels in the Puget Sound area.

While the modernization program was gaining momentum, new construction was also started during 1940. The passage of the Selective Service Act in August and the continually growing enlistment quotas meant that new selectees would soon be arriving for training. To meet the housing needs of these troops, the Quartermaster Corps embarked on a hurried building program at Casey and other forts within the Sound. Between the summer of 1940 and the end of 1941, twenty-five new buildings were erected at Fort Casey. These included nine two story barracks, three mess halls, two company storehouses, a post exchange, a theatre, an infirmary, new officer's quarters and an NCO club.

On August 27, 1940, Congress, after extended debate and with urgings from President Roosevelt, authorized the induction of the National Guard into the Regular Army and the calling up of the Army's Organized Reserves. On September 14th, the Selective Service and Training Act was also passed. These measures, together with an additional authorized increase in Regular Army strength, were designed to produce a 1,000,000-man army by the start of 1941 and 1,400,000 by July, 1941.[19]

In Puget Sound, this merged the 248th Washington National Guard into the 14th Coast Artillery. Manpower levels slowly began to increase, and throughout 1941 there was a slow but steady increase in both new men and work. The events of December 7, 1941 spurred troop increases even more as all the forts of Puget Sound began to feel the press of new recruits.

Just before the federalization of the National Guard in September, the Regular Army garrison at Fort Worden, then the only active post in the area, amounted to 30 officers and 600 enlisted men. Soon after, the increase in troops spread out to all forts, including the two new positions under construction: Striped Peak and Fort Ebey. The following shows manpower levels through the end of 1943:

DATE	Enlist. Men	Officers	Warr. Officers
31 January 1941	1,924	119	4
30 June 1941	2,928	169	5
7 December 1941	2,670	157	5
1 January 1942	3,288	165	4
30 June 1942	3,361	174	6
1 November 1942	3,638	206	6
31 December 1942	3,971	183	5
31 March 1943	4,221	188	12
30 June 1943	3,870	186	14
31 December 1943	3,360	182	15[20]

New troops began to arrive at Admiralty Head before the construction program had been completed. When Sergeant Roy Engom was transferred from Fort Worden near the end of 1940, only three of the barracks were completed enough to be used, so everyone was crowded into the few that were done. He recalled,

The fort in general was very well preserved from caretaker status. No dripping cement or leaking passageways. The original barracks had been torn down and the civilian contractor was building the new ones. The officer's quarters and enlisted men's quarters were there as was the post hospital. The guns

LEFT: Basic uniform for new troops arriving at Fort Casey in 1941. The fear of potential gas attacks led to the gas proofing all permanent structures. This included all plotting rooms, first aide stations, and of course, latrines.

RIGHT: The 1903 bolt action Springfield rifle was still standard as were the wrap leggings and breeches because of shortages. Only those divisional units facing prompt shipment into combat zones received newer equipment. The post storehouse is in the background with the newly constructed barracks on the right.

had been well cared for and were very serviceable. They were turned on their mounts once a week and the carriages were moved so they would stay balanced in their emplacements. The guns were never left in one position too long because of their tremendous weight. They were old and obsolete but they were all we had![21]

Private Richard Izban came to Casey from Worden in February of 1941. Like Engom he was crowded into one of the three completed barracks while work continued on the others.

I enlisted in Chicago, Illinois, and was assigned to the 14th Coast Artillery. We traveled for three days by train before we arrived in Seattle. We were tired and a little dirty when we got off the train at the ferry dock. Someone said we were in the Northwest and he was right. I stepped off the train and right into a puddle of water. Yep! We were in Washington. We were then sent by boat, the Virginia V, to Casey. We arrived at the fort at midnight with a suitcase in one hand and our barracks bag over the other shoulder. The regular Army men that met us woke us all up by telling everyone to be careful crossing the dark bridge from the dock to the road or we might fall into Crockett's Lake. We were double bunked in the barracks for 3 to 4 weeks. At night the barracks bags were put on the floor which made getting out of bed in the middle of the night risky at best. By March the other barracks were finished and the men were spread out.[22]

Another soldier on the train to Seattle with Dick Izban was Emerson Jedele. Like Isban he was originally drafted for one year but Pearl Harbor changed all that. After his late night arrival and dealing with the housing problems he was assigned to the mortars.

We started our training on the mortars. When I got there the guns weren't in the pits yet. They had been taken apart, completely coated in Cosmoline, and were stored in the magazine tunnels. A Sergeant Jacobson was in charge of assembling them. We spent days with boiling water and different solutions cleaning the parts. It took us about 10 weeks to assemble the 12 mortars and install them in the pits. Battery Schenck had all of its 8 mortars, 4 per pit, but Seymour only had two guns per pit. The front two had been removed. It is amazing to me how much we accomplished in those 10 weeks.[23]

By June of 1941, the troop population at Fort Casey was up to 400. Sentries now manned the posts two gates and walked the fortified zone along the shoreline. The parade grounds were being used for drill and formations and once again the guns of the fort were being used to train Coast Artillery troops.

The attack on Pearl Harbor found the United States Army and Coastal Defense still not as prepared as they should have been, despite after nearly a year and a half of mobilization. The Army and the forts of the Coast Defense were largely supplied with worn or obsolete equipment. New recruits were still being issued World War I choker collars, breeches, and wrap leggings as part of their uniforms. The 1903 bolt action Springfield rifle was still standard issue, and because of shortages, only divisional units facing prompt shipment into combat zones were to receive 100 percent of their authorized equipment. The Army suffered with shortages well into 1943. Even after the fall of France, Roosevelt continued to hesitate before a fully candid commitment either to the support England and France or to the rearmament of the United States.[24] The president was afraid that an abrupt redirecting of the national economy from domestic needs to the production of war materials was too much of an overt challenge to isolationism. He still had to be concerned over the political consequences.

The attack on Pearl Harbor solved the president's problems, concerning industrial commitment at least, and resolved the question of isolationism versus internationalism. The major problem now, as Malin Craig had warned in 1936, was the time it would take to get American industry mobilized and the resulting materials into the field. On December 7, 1941, the United States Army still lacked the strength to do little more than defend its own shores. In some locations, even that was questionable.

When word reached Casey of the Pearl Harbor sneak attack, there were four Batteries of the 1st Battalion, 14th Coast Artillery on station: Batteries A, B, C, and K, which was minus one detachment. The fort was immediately put on 24-hour alert and all troops on leave were recalled. Private Don Lee was in the last hours of a 30-day leave.

I got a call on the phone to where I was at in Coupeville to come back to base. I told them I had 12 more hours and I wasn't coming till then. I didn't know at the time what had happened at Pearl. Not long after a couple of soldiers came to the door and we left.[25]

Richard Izban had been on leave with his wife.

When we found out about the attack we really didn't panic because we didn't know how bad it was. I wasn't even sure where Hawaii was. When I got back to the fort the next morning the guard at the gate had his gun out to challenge me. After I had identified myself, he told me to get into my dress OD'S, get my gun, gas mask and go over to the supply room and get live ammo. They gave me 40 rounds of live ammunition, before we had the belts but no bullets. The base was put on 24 hour alert and it was very confusing. I was still so new to Casey I didn't know where everything was.[26]

Roy Engom was on the post when word was received of the attack. Much like the others he said there wasn't any real panic. "*We didn't know how bad things were. If we had there might have been panic. The fort went on full alert and we didn't know if we were going to be invaded or not.*"[27]

Shortly after the work on reinstalling the mortars was completed Emerson Jedele volunteered to be transferred to communication. He and three others were put in charge of the Switchboard and began training on its operation. Eventually all the telephone lines from the Fort Worden switchboard, via the underwater cable, were transferred over to Casey and soon everything going in or out of the Fort by telephone had to pass through their PBX-switchboard.

On Sunday morning, December 7th, I was on duty, and a friend of mine was down at the Quartermaster's Dock waiting to catch a ride to Seattle. I got a call from the dock. Paul was down there listening to music as he waited for the boat. I said, "What are you doing still there I thought you left a long time ago?" He told me the boat was late. When I asked why he said, "Because of war!"

ABOVE: On the night of June 21, 1942, a Japanese submarine surfaced off the mouth of the Columbia and fired nine rounds from its deck gun. This is one of the craters left from the shells impacting in the marshland in front of Fort Stevens. None of the shells hit the fort or anything of importance.

RIGHT: The troops at Fort Stevens posted this sign soon after the shelling. Note the camouflage netting over the gun emplacements.

I laughed and said, "What war is that?" He replied, "We've been attacked, listen to the radio. The Japanese have attacked Pearl Harbor!" When I heard the change in his voice I began to believe him and changed the channels on my radio until I caught the news. It was just like somebody punching you in the stomach.[28]

The alert status at Casey meant that there were troops now stationed at all gun emplacements at all times. One section of men lived in the barracks while another section was billeted at the emplacements themselves. Eventually, after the initial invasion scare subsided, temporary barracks were put up behind the emplacements. Until then, the men lived in the tunnels. Sergeant Engom, whose first assignment was at the mortars, recalled that tunnel living was not as bad as it would seem now. *"They weren't the dripping cold place you see now. They had stoves, lights and weren't too bad."*[29] Private Lee was of a much different opinion. His assignment after Pearl Harbor was with the 3-inch guns Battery Van Horne.

The first couple of nights they just gave us a couple of blankets and had us sleep out by the guns in case of attack. We weren't really prepared. I didn't like the tunnels at all. They were cold, wet stinking things. Even with stoves they were still drippy.[30]

After an assessment of the military situation in Hawaii, what amounted to a warning was sent to the defenses on the Pacific Coast. In essence, it stated that for the time being, the West Coast would have to look to its own defenses since there was really nothing to prevent a Japanese invasion. The Northwest, with its airplane factory and naval yard, had ample reason for alarm. The Coast Artillery at Admiralty Inlet thus was given the chief assignment of not only fighting off attacks by ships and defending the harbor defenses against air and commando raids, but the prevention of entry by enemy submarines into the Sound.[31] All this was to be done by coast artillery emplacements designed and armed with weapons from 1900.

In those first weeks of the War, Fort Casey was still undermanned and unable to carry out all the patrol and guard duties that were needed. Because of the fear of invasion, the miles of beaches on Whidbey Island that fronted Admiralty Inlet and Puget Sound were patrolled by civilians. Armed with deer rifles and shot guns these volunteers functioned as observers, airplane spotters and beach patrols. The troops at the base were busy manning the gun batteries, observation posts, and putting up the hundreds of yards of barbed wire around the perimeter of the post. Each night the fort would send out patrols in 3/4 ton trucks with .30 caliber machine guns to meet these civilian groups. This was continued up until the Fort was brought up to strength in the months after Pearl Harbor and the Army took over. Men were stationed at Deception Pass to guard beaches as well as to man mobile 90mm and 37mm guns in the area. There were also weapons carriers sent out to patrol the island, armed with .50 and .30 caliber machine guns.[32]

Early in January, 1942, a camouflage program was quickly begun. Troops at the fort with some help from the Corps of Engineers began with salvaged fishnet, wire, and $1,000 worth of paint. Battery Van Horne was covered with burlap woven netting and the road coming down from Battery Turman was partially covered with natural shrubbery. The mortar emplacements were painted with a mottled effect to match the surrounding landscape. Much to the dislike of the families living on the post, the housing on the north side of the parade ground, called the "line," had their bright yellow covered over with khaki. The AA batteries located in the middle of a field, however, were more difficult to conceal. Eventually, one of the guns had a building put up around it with a collapsible roof that blended in with the surrounding farm buildings. Another was surrounded by a log stockade and earth-filled slope, which was sodded with grass. The third gun was covered by netting. As time passed, more elaborate measures were taken by the troops. A dummy gun, constructed of wood and canvas, was placed conspicuously out in the field as a decoy. The big 10-inch guns at the main emplacements were also camouflaged for a while but eventually were deliberately left exposed to potentially draw attack away from Van Horne or other structures at the post.

As the immediate risk of attack subsided, the fort fell back into a routine of training and drill. The new recruits were given instruction in firing guns of all sizes, from hand guns to the 12-inch mortars. They also had training in fire control, communications, and the general order of discipline given to every new U. S. Army recruit. Men were assigned to different parts of the fort for periods of time as they were trained in various skills to develop a specialty.

Richard Izban's first assignment after his brief duty at Battery Van Horne was with the seacoast searchlight near the dock area. When this was removed, he was transferred to the Fire Command Center at the lighthouse. While at the Command Battery he was assigned to specialize in communication.

> *In this building there were telephone communications to all the batteries, guns or lights, on the post. There was a telephone booth to each battery. The building was below ground level except for the windows and these were shuttered for protection. Each level had a depth position finder (DPF) that was used to sight the range of targets 12 to 15 miles away. From this building the commanding officer would assign targets to specific batteries. During practice I would be given instructions as to the direction the target was traveling, was it going from left to right, approximately how many thousand yards away, how many stacks and so on. Everything we sighted was considered the enemy. A fishing boat was a destroyer and if we saw two of them it was a fleet. Practices went on almost every day but after a while this got to be a bit old. On nice sunny days we would drill for an hour and a half to two then we would sit outside and sun ourselves. Now every weekday the Princess Margarette would come by the fort on its trip to Vancouver. At about 11:25 to 11:30 it would steam by and toot its horn to salute the fort. None of us had enough money to own a wrist watch so we used the boat as our lunch call. We would put our shirts on and head to the barracks for lunch.[33]*

Sergeant Roy Engom's first assignment was with the 12-inch mortars.

> *We practice fired and trained on the guns daily. To save the guns themselves, the powder and shells, the weapons were fired with sub-caliber ammunition. We placed a 3-inch gun barrel inside the mortar to reduce the size of the bore so that 3-inch shells could be fired. The basic ammunition was fired only once a year. By using the sub-caliber ammo they could practice daily with the huge weapons. We could train with the guns in their proper fashion but just not shoot the large caliber, expensive ammo. Firing the mortars with full caliber ammunition was something to see and hear. I felt they were much*

ABOVE: The proposed relocation of the Anti-Aircraft batteries to the empty emplacements at Batteries Moore and Kingsbury. This aerial photo was taken in 1938 but the move was not completed until 1943. Note in the photo the main barracks have been removed, the white 'U' shaped foundations near Battery Van Horne, and the old cantonment buildings from WW I are still present above the mortar emplacements.

more impressive than the 10-inch rifles because of the pits they were in. You had to stand on your tip toes and keep your mouth open to relieve the pressure. The heat, the noise, and the concussion of the firing were really something you just don't ever forget. The concussion would slap your pants against your legs like someone hitting you with a soaking wet towel.[34]

Another soldier who was at the Casey during the early years of the war was Corporal Mel Bates. Originally from Sedro Woolley, Washington, he was drafted in May, 1941, and after basic training at Fort Worden, he was transferred to Admiralty Head. Because of his auto mechanic background, he was put in charge of the post Motor Pool.

When I got to Casey I was put in charge of the Motor Pool located behind the Quartermaster building. We didn't have a lift of any kind just a shed with three stalls. I did have lots of help. We needed the drive train out of a jeep one time so we just tipped it over on its side to get it. I was only a Corporal but I had complete charge of the motor pool and the issuing of any gas. This was a Specialists job so I got out of the basic drills and military discipline that the rest of the men at the fort had to go through. My only real requirement was to be present for breakfast each morning and then it was back to the pool. I was in charge of and worked on all the motor vehicles at the camp. They were all GMC trucks and jeeps. Any vehicle that broke down was brought to me for repair.[35]

Billie Smith, one of Sergeant Nelson's daughters, who was raised at Casey, remembered the war bringing a lot of changes to her young life on the post.

My dad came home and told us about the attack on Pearl Harbor and that we had to keep everything dark. I don't remember any real panic for the adults when the war started but it sure was scary for us kids. There were black outs, air raid drills, and gas attack drills. During these drills we were taken out of the school, in Coupeville, and would walk to nearby farms for safety. The school was small enough that every kid had a place to go in the event of an attack. They would not try to get them back to the fort but instead to a safe home. It seems silly to me now but that's what they thought was best. Gas mask drills were the worst. We all had to put masks on and go down to the basement. I hated it. I was scared of the mask and how it felt to wear it. Life at the fort got very strict. There was barbed wire all over the place including the beach where we used to play and we had to stay away from the soldiers. We didn't know if the Japanese were coming on or over the water. Since we were living in a house overlooking the Inlet I was very frightened for a long time.[36]

The fear of invasion and bombing by the Japanese continued during 1942. Night firing drills were held regularly as were air raid and gas attack drills. There was also a strict black-out rule enforced. All the vehicles on the post, as well as those of civilians on the Island who were out after dark, had to be fitted with what were called "cats eyes." Car head lights were covered except for a small bar that was colored yellow. This strip was only visible to an oncoming car and in essence you were driving completely in the dark. Corporal Bates, who's job it was to put the first 500 miles on all new vehicles coming to Casey, spoke of making regular night drives across the Island and after a while, being able to do it pretty fast. "I could really fly from the Fort to Deception Pass until the Navy base went in. Then I got stopped by the Marines from the base and ticketed for speeding."[37]

On the night of June 21st, 1942, the fear of attack from the Japanese was brought home to the soldiers and families of the Northwest when a submarine surfaced off the mouth of the Columbia and opened fire. A little before 11:30 p.m., Submarine 1-25 fired 9 shells from its 5.5-inch deck gun at Fort Stevens from 10 miles off shore. Fort Stevens' guns--its newest installed in 1904--were unable to return fire. This was the first hostile shelling of a military base on the United States mainland since the War of 1812, and with the additional news that the Japanese had invaded the Aleutian Islands in Alaska at about the same time, the invasion anxiety in the Northwest increased.[38] Private Dick Izban, stationed at Headquarters Battery by the lighthouse, had his own take on this incident.

> *The officer put in charge of the modernization program and command of the Pacific Northwest was Brigadier General James Cunningham. Jumping, jittery, Jimmy, as he was called, saved the country a lot of money, like it was coming out of his own pocket. When the Japanese sub fired at Fort Stevens this was under Pacific Northwest control. He got the message of what was happening by telegraph key. If he told them to return fire it would have made the whole area a designated War Zone. In a war zone every serviceman in the area would have gotten a 20% increase in salary for combat pay. We all heard the reasons; that the sub submerged before they could return fire, it was out of range, they had no way to locate where it was, that they didn't want to give away the positions of the guns and so on. We just figured it was Jimmy saving money*[39]

The Modernization Program, begun in 1941, continued throughout 1942 and into 1943. Construction was well underway at the Striped Peak and Ebey's Landing locations, and roads were being cut for the Cape Flattery batteries. Railway mounted mortars, which could be quickly moved via commercial tracks, were installed at Angeles Point. Other moveable weapons, mobile 155mm, 90mm, and 37mm guns, were placed throughout the Puget Sound area primarily as anti-aircraft defenses. The twelve batteries of guns that had been ordered reconditioned for immediate use had been completed in early 1942 and were now in service. Anti-submarine nets were installed near the entrance to Bremerton and at the dock area of Port Townsend. In May the Navy assumed the responsibilities for the fixed underwater listening stations at Greenbank and Marrowstone Island. The Number 11 searchlight from Casey was transferred to the Greenbank station for service. An underwater magnetic loop early warning system was also being installed by the Navy off Point Wilson. Consisting of overlapping strands of armored copper, the cables were to be strung out in the entrance and would send back readings when ships passed over. The loops were so sensitive that they could pick up the slightest change in the earth's magnetic field caused by the steel hull of a ship. Additional plans were underway for the placement of an "ASDIC" (underwater echo ranging) system and the placement of SCR-296, surface craft detectors, in the Admiralty Inlet area.[40]

While these improvements were being made in the defenses of the Northwest, the vast majority of the pre-World War I big guns were being declared outmoded. As the new batteries were completed, the older guns of Admiralty Inlet were taken out of service and excluded from the modernization program. Initially this included all batteries at Fort Casey except Van Horne. This was changed,

ABOVE: Until the relocation of the post-WW I AA batteries was completed, the guns and the coincidence range finders used in targeting were manned by the new troops at Fort Casey. This was located in a field below the BOQ quarters near the site of the Balloon hanger. Pipe smoking was obviously very popular.

BELOW: Soldiers relaxing from training in front of the newly built barracks facing the parade ground. This housing was quickly completed to provide quarters for the hundreds of recruits arriving after the start of the war. Some men commented that you could hang your uniform on the nails sticking through the green wood.

however, as the need for firepower of any kind was called for in case of invasion. As the tide of Japanese advance was stopped at the Battle of the Coral Sea and Midway, a number of the big guns were declared outmoded. This included Batteries Moore, Worth, and Kingsbury. Meanwhile, construction on the Ebey's Landing battery neared completion. The remaining guns in service at Casey, mortar Batteries Seymour and Schenck, were also taken out of service. The newer guns being installed had ranges of fire far exceeding the now-ancient weapons of the turn of the century and were not as vulnerable to air attack.

A number of suggestions were made as to the potential use of these old weapons in other locations overseas but eventually the cost of removal, their age, and the need for scrap metal by a growing American war industry led to a final decision to salvage. In October, all the remaining guns at Fort Casey, except for the two 3-inch guns at Van Horne, were placed on the list of batteries "No longer required." The Salvage of Obsolete Armament Movement, as it was officially called, swept through Puget Sound, ravaging all the Inlet forts. By October 24, 1942, the last of Casey's original large caliber armament had been cut up and hauled away by barge.

With the removal of the original guns and the need for a better location for the AA battery at Casey, it was decided to move the mobile guns from the field below the mortars up to the now empty gun pits of Battery Kingsbury and Moore. The movement of the guns began in September of 1942 and was completed by the end of June, 1943. The three 3-inch antiaircraft guns were placed atop Kingsbury 1 & 2 and Moore 3. Part of the rooms under the old gun emplacements were converted for use as quarters, rest rooms and ammunition storage.[41] Sergeant Roy Engom had been transferred to the new AA battery with the removal of the mortars from active service. He remembered seeing the guns being cut up.

> *It was kind of sad. We were training on the 3-inch guns while the 10-inchers were being cut up with blow torches. They sliced up the guns, their carriages, and even the iron railing around the emplacements. A virtual sweep of the fort was made of metal. It seemed like a shame to just cut them up but we really couldn't have done much with the guns anyway. There was also a fair amount of theft occurring by people sneaking in and stealing the scrap metal.*[42]

Records show that by the end of the year all of the original guns at Casey save the rapid fire 3-inch guns at Battery Van Horne were gone.

The scrap metal drive that took the last of the heavy weapons at Casey also affected other parts of the fort. Corporal Jedele was now in charge of the switchboard crew. He and the other three men now manned the communication center 24 hours a day with rotating shifts. There were always two men on duty at all times in the underground bunker. To save time the men moved out of the main barracks and bunked in the old radio room across the road.

> *I spent most of my free time at the Switchboard and became a sort of jack of all trades helping my sergeant at fixing things. All the wiring at the fort was the same as was installed for WWI, heavy lead cables in underground tubes wrapped in metal sheathing. As the scrap drives were going, they began to remove some of the useless lead cables as there was a real shortage of lead. I would accompany Sergeant*

Stillwell to certain manhole covers and we would remove the old lines and cut them up with backsaws into manageable lengths for scrap. It was terrible work because of the lead and the metal wrapping around it. We broke many back saw blades.[43]

In 1943, the defenses against air attack (AA) and surface raids by small vessels (AMTB) reached their highest state of development. The installation of new batteries of mobile and fixed 37mm and 90mm armament and the repositioning of older 3-inch AA batteries, such as at Casey, provided greater defense in depth. By mid-1943 the project listed the following positions under its command:

Deception Pass	2-mobile 90mm
Ebey's Landing	2-fixed 90mm
Fort Worden	2-fixed and 2 mobile 90mm
Fort Flagler	2-fixed and 2 mobile 90mm, 3 fixed 3-inch AA/AMTB guns
Fort Casey	2-mobile 90mm, 3 fixed 3-inch AA/AMTB and 37mm guns
Point Hudson, Port Townsend	2-37mm guns
Ediz Hook, Port Angeles	2-37mm guns
Portage Channel	1-37mm gun
Agate Passage	3-37mm guns
Rich Passage	2-37mm guns
Fort Whitman	2-37mm guns
Bremerton	4-37mm guns

Note: the 37mm and mobile 99mm guns also had AA capabilities.[44]

Also during 1943, radar was first introduced to the area. Stations were located at Forts Worden, Casey and the soon to be completed, Fort Ebey. These stations were a big improvement on the magnetic loops and more versatile than the tower-mounted SCR 296 surface craft detector system. At Admiralty Head, a large trailer-mounted, mobile unit arrived in May, 1943. Powered by a gas generator, the unit was set up in the grass field area behind the main emplacement. The only problem was that when the equipment arrived there was nobody trained to operate it. No technicians were sent with the system because there were not any in the area. The technology was just too new.

Sergeant Roy Engom was assigned to this new unit and helped to assemble it following instructions in the technical manuals that were included. The men had basic knowledge in electronics but nothing else.

We got it going without much trouble but we weren't sure what we were seeing. We would get readings from the mountains and didn't know what it was. We would pick up a bird and everybody

ABOVE: Morning calisthenics on the parade ground in front of the barracks. Some of the newly arriving troops are still housed in tents, visible in the background. The white structure in the upper right is the small arms firing range.

BELOW: Part of Emerson Jedele's crew working in the Switchboard. Two men were on duty at all times to monitor all communications in and out of the fort.

would run out to see what it was, a plane or what. We put in a request to get a plane to fly over so we could see just what a blip on the scope looked like. It was just a completely new thing and we had to figure it out through the manuals and by experimenting. It was a revolving type of radar that was mounted on a truck. Everything was powered by a gas generator.

They finally sent someone to tech school to learn about it and when he came back they set up a school to teach others. They still kept the range finders and direction locators at the fort. They were back up if the radar failed.[45]

As conditions of the war shifted in favor of the allies and the threat of invasion ended, a re-evaluation of the harbor defense program nation-wide was made. Construction on a number of large and small gun emplacements along the Pacific Coast was stopped. In Washington, work at the two Cape Flattery locations was discontinued in August, 1943, and plans for 6-inch batteries at Tongue Point, Koitlah Point and Ocean Creek on the peninsula were all abandoned. Fort Ebey, however, was completed during the year. Work continued at the 16-inch battery at Striped Peak.[46]

At Fort Casey, the removal of the big guns left the main job of the fort to now be one of drill and training. The troops were trained in a wide variety of fields which provided an unusually thorough background for the men of the Coast Artillery. The men received instruction in gas warfare, communications, the use of searchlights, small arms, ballistics, machine guns and, of course, the larger guns still in place. The 3-inch rapid fire guns of Battery Van Horne and the 3-inch battery of antiaircraft guns now atop the empty main emplacements provided training in larger weapons. There were continual drills and practice firings as well as accuracy competitions between the other forts of the Inlet. Roy Engom remembered:

In the mornings we drilled the men on the guns. After morning practices the afternoons were taken up with the more mundane tasks; drilling, upkeep of the fort grounds, and the tasks of every army post. Monday evenings were used for night firing practice. In these practices, under lights, all the normal conditions were practiced. When the weather was bad the men were put through classes in ordnance and other skills of ballistics. The training was constant and the men were the best. They were trained in ordnance as well as being Infantry. After four years of nothing but practice we became pretty good.[47]

Private Don Lee, who had been assigned to the newly positioned AA Battery, remembered target practice during 1943.

I was part of a three gun battery on top of the old Kingsbury emplacement. The gun had originally been out in the field behind the mortars. They had hand cranks for elevation and were connected to the range finders. I had to be quick to check the range and yell fire. We were all pretty much idiots because we didn't wear any kind of ear protection. We could probably fire 2 to 3 shots a minute. On Fridays we would have live practice at a wind sock type target pulled by a plane from Paine Field. The three guns crews would compete against each other. We would dip the 3-inch AA shells into different cans of paint to color the tips before we loaded them for firing. If the shell passed through the wind sock it would leave a trail of paint and we could tell who had scored the most hits. One time after the plane pulling the target had made a couple of passes the pilot apparently thought we were getting too close to him and radioed that he wasn't coming back. It seems one of our shots had cut the cable fairly close to the tail of the plane. I knew exactly where I was going every Friday afternoon.[48]

Another soldier who was stationed at Admiralty Head during 1943 was Private Donald Sutton, a transfer from Camp Roberts, California, assigned to the seacoast searchlights. After two months of what Sutton considered really boring duty, he took the opportunity to transfer to a new specialization at the forts of the Inlet - K-9 sentry duty.

They came around one day asking if anyone wanted to work with dogs and since I disliked working with the lights I took the offer. Our job was patrolling the dock area with dogs during the night. The dogs were trained in California and brought up to Casey and the other forts. A sergeant who came with them instructed us on how to use them. The dogs were trained to just alert sentries and not attack. At Casey we had a German shepherd, a golden retriever who wasn't much good, and a Doberman pincher who was afraid of his own shadow. At night the CO would come around and check on you and the pincher would be asleep or standing behind you. We got rid of him pretty quick. Other than that dog the rest were really pretty good. The dogs were very good at alerting us that someone was coming down the hill from the NCO Club or coming to check up on us. Our duty was for 48 hours on and 72 hours off, our work time from 5 p.m. to 8 a.m. and we worked in four hour shifts. Because our work was all at night everyone in the detail were moved out of the regular barracks and into the empty lighthouse. We had our own mess and didn't have to worry about trying to sleep during the day with men coming and going like it would be in the regular barracks. We had it pretty easy and we knew it.[49]

Private Sutton spoke very highly of the quality of men stationed at Fort Casey during his stay. This was also the view of Sergeant Engom, Corporal Bates, and Privates Izban and Lee. The regular soldiers of the Coast Artillery serving at Fort Casey were praised for their efficiency, their skill in handling men, their knowledge and the loyalty they had for the Army. They were "lifers," as the men called them, professional soldiers. Corporal Bates was very impressed with them. *"I felt it was a privilege to train with them. You could drill with them all day and not get bored. They really knew their business and loved the Army and what it stood for."*[50] Richard Izban remembered one sergeant who considered the Army his wife. *"If you said something bad about the Army the Sergeant would ask you to come over to the gym after dinner for a little boxing workout. You learned very quickly not to speak against the Army."*[51] With this quality of training, the men of the Coast Artillery maintained the reputation begun during World War I of being among the best trained troops in the Army.

By 1944, the suspense of World War II was substantially over. Barring unforeseen developments, it was only a matter of time before the Allied rings would finally close around Germany and Japan.[52] The suspense was also over for Fort Casey and the forts of the Coast Defense. With the tide of battle moving further and further away from the Pacific Coast, the fort was used primarily as a training station for troops heading overseas. The advent of air power had brought to an end the practical usefulness of Coast Artillery as designed at the turn of the century. Forts like Casey, Worden

LEFT: The Fort Casey Motor Pool located behind the Quartermaster's Storehouse. This was the work area of Corporal Mel Bates. He was in charge of service and repair of all vehicles at the post.

BELOW: The upper gate at Fort Casey. Corporal Emerson Jedele pretending he was on guard duty for the picture.

and Flagler would continue to serve the Army adequately as training facilities but as defensive fortifications they were useless.

With each month, more and more of the original Coast Artillery troops were shipped out. The flow of new recruits began to slow during the early months of 1944; the entire Puget Sound Harbor Defense saw its manpower levels drastically fall during the year. The transfer of men to Europe and the Pacific theatre continued, but now there were no replacements following along behind. Training did continue during 1944. In June Battery G was transferred to Casey from Fort Worden for special commando exercises. A specialized training course was built in the woods behind the lighthouse, and the troops of this unit were prepared for commando-type missions. Their training completed, in September, the unit was returned to Worden.[53]

On October 17, 1944 General Order Number 80 was received by the Western Defense Command and was in turn sent out to the Headquarters of the Harbor Defense of the Puget Sound. The order disbanded the 14th Coast Artillery. A re-organization took place and the men of the 14th were divided among three new battalions of Coast Artillery. One battalion was assigned to Forts Ebey and Casey, one to the completed Striped Peak battery now named Camp Hayden and one to Fort Worden. All were reduced considerably in strength. This came only six months after the transfer of the 248th Coast Artillery, which along with the 14th had been responsible for Harbor Defense in Puget Sound, to Camp Barkley, Texas. The reorganization of the Coast Artillery brought re-designations to all the Batteries and the transferring of a great many men. For Fort Casey it was the beginning of the end.

As 1944 proceeded, more and more of the veteran soldiers who had come to Admiralty Head during the 1941-42 buildup were being transferred out or had already left. Private Don Lee departed in 1943. He described it as, *"Getting a wild hair on my butt and decided to join the Infantry."*[54] Private Richard Izban had been transferred to Worden in mid-1942 and would eventually end up in Alaska. Sergeant Roy Engom was one of the large number of men who was transferred out when the Coast Artillery reorganized in 1944. He also went into the Infantry. After the war he would return to the area as the caretaker at Fort Ebey. Corporal Mel Bates, like Lee, decided he wanted to see some action and also went into the Infantry. He ended up in Europe and found a great deal of what he was looking for in Belgium during the "Battle of the Bulge." Corporal Emerson Jedele left Casey in February, 1944, despite the shortage of trained men to operate the Switchboard. As the fort was closing down he was sent to Texas and Boston, and then put on a boat headed for Europe. While enroute the war in Europe ended(VE day) and this sent the boat in a different direction. Fortunately the war in the Pacific ended (VJ Day) while Corporal Jedele's boat was on the way to the Pacific theater.

Private Donald Sutton remained stationed at Fort Casey until late 1944. He was part of one of the last group of men to leave as the fort was being closed down. Most were sent to Worden and then to Seattle to secure transportation to their new Infantry units. He returned after the War in 1946 to see Fort Casey again and found it very different.

There was only 1 man in charge of the place. He and his family were responsible for the entire fort. All the officer's quarters were empty and all the guns had been removed. The main barracks were all boarded up and the gates unmanned. Everything was closed up.[55]

The end of World War II in September of 1945 found the manpower levels in the Puget Sound at their lowest since 1941. From a high of 4,221 enlisted men in March of 1943, the Harbor Defense listed only 1,065 men under its command on September 16, 1945. Forts Casey, Flagler, Ward, Whitman and Camp Hayden had all been de-activated and were under caretaker status. Once again, weeds took over the parade ground and buildings were left to weather. The Coast Artillery had outlived its usefulness and Fort Casey, like dozens of other coastal defense installations in the United States, was no longer needed. Nevertheless, it had again been a functional part of the national defense.

Between 1940 and 1945 almost one-quarter of a billion dollars had been consumed on harbor defense programs in the United States.[56] Like other defense programs begun during other wars, many of the planned projects were never completed; of the more than 150 batteries projected during World War II, about two-thirds were brought to structural completion. Despite the fact that Fort Casey had been constructed, for the most part, before 1900 and was still using weapons from that same period, the attack on Pearl Harbor brought it back into service. It would again serve the nation well. Despite its age and obvious vulnerabilities, it was still part of an American harbor defense system that by 1944 had become the most extensive and formidably armed system of seacoast defenses in our nation's history.[57] Though old and gray as the cement of the emplacement walls, it still served a valuable purpose during the War, and as in 1918, the residents of Whidbey Island were glad it was there.

ABOVE: On Sunday, August 11, 1968, the last two remaining 10-inch disappearing rifles left in the world were dedicated at Fort Casey. Senator Henry M. Jackson and Governor Daniel J. Evans were in attendance as was the Washington National Guard Band. It had taken over seven years of work, thousands of dollars of donated and legislated money, and hundreds of volunteers, but Fort Casey once more had its guns.

CHAPTER SEVEN

1945 to the Present

In the years immediately after the end of World War II, Fort Casey continued to function as a part of the military establishment of Puget Sound. Like the other forts of the old Harbor Defense system, however, Fort Casey's days of usefulness as a coastal defense installation were over. The technology of modern warfare developed during the war had shown the whole concept of harbor defense by long range artillery to be no longer practical. The techniques of amphibious invasion and aerial bombardment made it unnecessary to secure port facilities for invasion and thus the importance of harbor defense was gone. A few of the coastal defense projects that were close to finishing before VJ Day or not finished by war's end were allowed to reach completion, but by 1948 they too were being phased out and their guns removed. A good example of this was the Angeles Point or Striped Peak 16" gun battery located on the Strait of Juan de Fuca, about 15 miles west of Port Angeles, Washington. Work began on this installation in October 1942 with its intended field of fire covering not only the entrance to Puget Sound but also the approaches to the harbor of Victoria, British Columbia, and the Canadian naval base at Esquimalt. It was completed in May of 1945 with construction continuing even though the progress of the war had long since eliminated its need. The battery was commissioned into service, test fired twice, and then decommissioned on the same day. Work then began on dismantling the facility. The gun and its carriage were later sold as scrap.

By 1949 the last of the guns at the major harbors such as Boston, New York, and San Francisco had been scrapped. Not long afterward, at the beginning of 1950, the remaining harbor defense commands were disbanded, and the seacoast fortifications of the United States passed into history.[1]

At Admiralty Head, a small garrison of men initially was assigned to maintain the fort as a satellite facility of the still-active Fort Worden. Although there was very little done to care for the buildings or to restrict the public from access, the post was, nevertheless, still Army property and as such had to be manned. The remaining guns left at the fort were removed soon after the war. The three 3-inch antiaircraft guns, of Fixed AA Number 1 that had been relocated from the fields below the mortars to the main emplacements in 1943, were dismantled in the early part of 1946. Somewhat ironically, the last weapons to leave were part of the original armament installed at the turn of the century. The two pedestal mounted, 3-inch rapid fire rifles of Battery Isaac Van Horne, installed in 1905, were salvaged by June -- the last of Fort Casey's teeth officially pulled.

From 1946 through 1949, serving as a sub-installation of Fort Worden, Fort Casey was used periodically as a training area for Engineer battalions stationed across the Inlet. After the war, Fort Worden, as the only active fort of the old Coast Defense, continued to serve as a training area for Amphibious Engineer units that would practice landings on the beaches at Admiralty Head, Marrowstone Island and Point Wilson. The new technology of amphibious invasion that had been part of the downfall of the Coast Artillery was now being taught within sight of the old emplacements.

Between 1946 and the start of 1950, Fort Casey was kept on the list of Active Army Installations, but in name only. By the end of 1946, the garrison at Admiralty Head consisted of one family living in one of the Officers' quarters. There was, however, occasional activity. A number of the buildings erected in the building boom of World War II were removed, including the Post Exchange, the Infirmary, the NCO Club, the Radio location shelter (SCR268), and some small ancillary structures. The post water system was being maintained by the still present Sergeant Nelson, as he and his family were now living in the old pumping station.

Some new construction did take place during 1947-48 but did not actually affect the fort itself. A tract of approximately 12 acres at the dock area was designated for a permanent ferry landing. It had been approved by the Secretary of War in 1941, but it was not until 1947 that the Corps of Engineers began work. The facility became the Keystone Harbor Ferry Slip and Small Boat Basin and is still maintained by the Corps today. Of a more direct effect on the fort was the first sale of reservation property. In November, 1948, the government declared part of the Casey Reservation as surplus real property and put it up for public sale. Two tracts of land on the old Brooklyn Town site along the beach opposite Crockett's Lake were sold for $7,796. The tracts contained 22.96 acres and 3 buildings.

In the latter part of 1949 the fort received some real activity, as one of the Engineer Battalions from Fort Worden was moved to Admiralty Head for training. The 56th Amphibious Tank and Tractor Battalion, some 600 men, were transferred across the Inlet and once more Fort Casey came alive. A number of the barracks and support buildings were reopened; new concrete roadways were installed to accommodate the amphibious tanks. The old balloon hangar support buildings were used for storage of the vehicles, and for a few months, the lower portion of the 50 year old fort was again a bee hive of activity.

A civilian electrician who worked at the fort during this period was Coupeville native Daryl Franzen. He had been a jack-of-all-trades while in the Army and applied for work when the Amphibious Battalion was transferred from Worden. His duties were to repair switches, replace lights, install new chimneys, keep the furnaces running, and solve any electrical problems.

> *I was Civil Service so I didn't associate much with the military. I just took care of the electrical problems. They were only using 3 or 4 of the barracks and a couple of the mess halls. All of the buildings were using coal for heating. The old central power plant was not used at all. I remember watching them practice amphibious landings on the beaches in front of the lighthouse. They said they could go anywhere with those tanks. Then one day someone had the bright idea of taking one of the tanks and trying to cross Crockett's Lake. About 50 yards from shore the tank got stuck and started to sink. They worked for hours trying to get the tank unstuck but nothing worked. They finally had to go to one of the local farmers and have him bring his draft horse team. The horses were eventually able to pull the tank loose. The farmer and his sons thought it was pretty funny. I am not so sure the officer in charge did.[2]*

By April 17, 1950, the third rebirth of Fort Casey was over. On that day, the Army announced that the 56th Battalion was being transferred to Fort Flagler and that Fort Casey was being placed in caretaker status. The reasons given for the change were the lack of modern training facilities, the swiftness of the current through the Inlet, which made it very difficult for the tanks to cross, and the age-old cry of economy.[3] Less than three months later the final chapter was closed, as the Coast Artillery was officially abolished as a separate branch of the Army. The Coast Artillery, which was now totally anti-aircraft, was recombined with those of the Field Artillery into a single Artillery branch. The twenty-year history of the Coast Artillery had come to an end.

Even before this closing of the Coast Artillery and the inactivation of Fort Casey took place, local residents and newspapers were beginning to take notice. Editorials from the Whidbey Farm

LEFT: Following the end of the war and the decommissioning of Fort Casey, many of the buildings and emplacements were left to weather and deteriorate in the salt air. The top of the light was removed for future restoration and the tower was sealed, but the rest of the structure was left unattended. It was only through the efforts of the State Parks and local civic groups that the lighthouse was saved.

BEOW: Many of the wood buildings were just boarded up and left to gradually decline in the elements. The near building was the Engineer's quarters across from the present day Ranger's home with one of the NCO's quarters in the distance. Both were removed due to safety concerns.

Bureau News began to appear, calling for some action to save the once proud military post.

> *We have become so occupied with the future of the naval air station here and the closing of Seattle's Sandpoint base, that we have overlooked a complete closure of a military installation virtually in our own back yard. Once proud Fort Casey, for the last month has been steadily drained of its life's blood as troops stationed there have been transferred to other posts on the Sound. By May 10, the historic post, which has stood guard over the western shores of Whidbey for 50 years, will pass into retirement. All that will remain of the many hundreds of men stationed there will be a crew of caretakers who will stay on until final disposition of the fort. The Army said there is no longer need of Fort Casey. The sharp, cruel knife of economy has cut and slashed another famed fortification to tatters.*
>
> *Always a favorite post to Army men, Casey and Coupeville beckoned many of them to return when their services for their country were no longer needed. They hastened home to spend the remainder of their lives, here on the island near the fort. Surely there must be some way to revive this fort that has meant much to Whidbey. Let us now return past favors by striving to encourage the retention of the fort in some military capacity. We don't want to see it put on the auction block after June 30 at a surplus sale.*[4]

Soon after Casey was placed in caretaker status, the custody of the reservation was placed with the Seattle District, Corps of Engineers. The Army now was free to remove its few remaining troops, and the Corps of Engineers took responsibility for the maintenance of the fort. For the next four years, the fort remained under the administration of the Corps with a monthly custodial cost of about $1,150. This definitely was not spent on upkeep of the majority of the posts buildings. Admiralty Head again returned to its ghost town state, with only the occasional curious visitor wandering about the abandoned emplacements.

On April 20, 1954, the Corps of Engineers transmitted to the General Services Administration (GSA) a report that declared the majority of the Fort Casey Military Reservation to be excess to the known defense needs of the Department of Defense.[5] Other than the small acreage set aside for the ferry slip and 1.7 acres reserved by the Coast Guard for a possible future navigational aid, the remainder of Fort Casey, close to 500 acres, was declared surplus and would be sold as such. This raised a mild cry of protest from local citizens, including a number of Casey veterans who had returned to live in the local area. Editorials again appeared in the local Oak Harbor and Coupeville newspapers calling on the Army to keep the fort in some capacity, but nothing was accomplished. The forts of Admiralty Inlet were being disposed of and local editorials were not going to stop it. Fort Flagler was de-activated in June of 1953 and finally Fort Worden was closed on June 22, 1955.

For the next two years the majority of the fort was unused and uncared for. A few of the officer's quarters and the lighthouse were boarded up but the rest of the fort and most of the land was almost completely open. The question now arose as to what would happen to Fort Casey. Sections of the reservation along Crockett's Lake and on the outlying areas of the reservation were sold off to private citizens, but the main portion containing the majority of the buildings and the old emplacements remained.

In opening the land for sale, the General Services Administration (GSA) gave some agencies and institutions preference toward the purchase of the more important sections of the fort. State Departments such as the State Game and the State Parks were given an opportunity to buy, as were schools in the state. During 1955-56, two of these potential buyers engaged in something of a struggle over the old fort. Seattle Pacific College, in Seattle, and the State Parks Commission were both interested in obtaining land and, for a time, both were vying for the same property.

Once the fort had been declared surplus, local residents and service clubs began actively soliciting the State Parks Commission to purchase some or all the fort for use as a future state park. The Coupeville Lions Club, in particular, lobbied for the entire reservation to be bought as a park. As luck would have it, a member of the Parks Commission, John Vanderzicht, lived in nearby Oak Harbor and was interested in the idea. While this was happening, Seattle Pacific College was also showing interest in buying land to use as a retreat/summer camp-type facility. This set up somewhat of a conflict, particularly in the Coupeville area, as some residents favored the church (Seattle Pacific is a Methodist church sponsored school located in Seattle) getting the land. Eventually, both sides obtained land but low key conflict between the church and state went on.

Through the work of John Vanderzicht and the State Parks Commission, 110 acres of the Fort Casey Reservation was leased for use as a future state park on December 2, 1955. Under the Surplus Property Act of 1944 and the Federal Property & Administration Services Act of 1949, the State could lease the land permanently as long as they agreed to the continuous use and maintenance of the land and its structures as an historic monument and for the benefit of the public. This was done by the Washington State Parks Department and Island County with the filing of a Quit Claim deed on December 2. The deed was for twenty years and was renewed in 1975 and again in 1995. Also reserved in this agreement was .83 acres at the ferry terminal by the Corps of Engineers. The Keystone Ferry Slip and Harbor were to be maintained by the Corps on a permanent basis and still are today. The State thus took possession of 110 acres containing 13 buildings of various types and the former gun emplacements of Batteries Trevor, Valleau, Kingsbury, Moore, Worth, Schenck, Seymour, Van Horne, and Turman. The acreage also included tidelands and sea beds extending 1/4 mile out from the shoreline. A very small piece of land on the southernmost tip of Admiralty Head was also reserved by the Coast Guard for possible use as an aid to navigation, but this was included in the 110 acres lease. The land was now considered an historic monument and its future was considerably more secure.[6]

Seattle Pacific continued its efforts to purchase land and on June 29, 1956, the school obtained 40 acres for the price of $42,000. The section contained all of the barracks, mess halls, officers' quarters and the entire parade ground. A few years later, 160 more acres adjoining the original purchase and running north toward the upper end of the reservation were donated to the college. A local resident named Bocker deeded the land he had purchased from the GSA to the school at his death. This brought the Seattle Pacific holdings to 200 acres.[7]

The City of Coupeville also benefited from the surplus declaration by purchasing the water system at the fort for approximately $12,000. It consisted of 18 wells, the pump house, the pump house residence and a 500,000 gallon reservoir. The system is still in use today, although the pump house residence was moved into Coupeville in 1960 and became the Town Hall.[8] Although Fort Casey's days as a coastal defense installation were over, there were other uses that it was destined to fill. Besides its

LEFT: This secondary battery observation station was located along the spit by Crockett's Lake. It suffered not only from lack of care but, like much of the fort that was left unattended, from vandalism. It eventually had to be removed for public safety.

RIGHT: This shot of the range and meteorological stations located on the small hill behind the main emplacements shows the results from lack of proper care. The roofs which were part glass slowly succumbed to the weather and vandalism and had to be removed. Today the interior can only be viewed through plexiglas coverings.

use as a state park and as a church camp it would soon also serve the public as a shelter. As early as 1954, the concrete tunnels were being considered for Civil Defense fallout shelters.[9]

On September 22, 1949, President Harry Truman issued a statement: "We have evidence that within recent weeks an atomic explosion occurred in the U.S.S.R."[10] With this act, the Soviet Union ended the American monopoly of the atom and brought to a sudden end the era of seeming American invincibility that had begun at Hiroshima. In the years that followed the Russian emergence into the Atomic Age, America began thinking about civil defense. The history of Civil Defense that followed was characterized by fits and spurts of activity but never was it totally accepted or supported by the people or the government. The potential danger to the American public from radioactive fallout began to be taken seriously, at least by some, by 1954, as both the U.S. and Russia were testing large-yield nuclear weapons in the atmosphere. While the government put its faith and support in the concept of "massive retaliation" as a deterrent, the beginning steps of organizing a shelter system in America began.

In the Northwest, Civil Defense was primarily concerned with protection from fallout. County directors were selected throughout the state and the search for adequate shelters began. Fort Casey, with its massive concrete and earthen-lined tunnels, seemed a logical choice for the Island County area. In the fall of 1954, the state was given permission from the Federal Government, which still owned the reservation, to use the bunkers at Casey for fallout protection. This permission continued after the upper portion of the fort was purchased by the state in 1955. All supplies used for stocking the tunnels for CD were distributed by the Federal Government. This was surplus material from WW II and the Korean conflict. The first Island County Civil Defense Director was Roy Evans.

> *The Civil Defense headquarters for the local area was located in Oak Harbor and as the first director I worked to make use of the Casey tunnels. When I took over in 1954 it was a constant struggle to get support and money. The only real change in attitude came when the county found it could buy GSA (Government Surplus Properties) surplus for nominal fees. We could get everything that we felt we needed from the Feds to use for civil defense. We purchased food, vehicles, medicine, general equipment and such for next to nothing. In 1958 we selected the mortar tunnels and mortar headquarters command building for our CD shelters. The fort was not being cared for at all and the tunnels were just filthy. We were able to get a group of Marines from the Naval Air Base in Oak Harbor to come over and help clean the bunkers out. To raise money to equip the tunnels we decided to have a dance and what better place to stage it than inside them. We organized the event to have a different type band, jazz, ballroom, modern, in each of the first three tunnels. We brought in a water buffalo, strung electrical cable for lights, brought in an electric generator, and had 40 watt bulbs every 15 feet inside, all purchased from surplus. We advertised all over the area but didn't really know how many people might show up so you can understand how amazed we were when over 1,500 came. Everyone had a ball. The only problem was that we didn't charge enough and when it came time to pay off all our bills we ended up $40 in the hole. The dance pretty much characterized Civil Defense in the United States, a lot of interest but no real money or support.[11]*

For the next 16 years, the tunnels at Casey were used as the primary fallout shelters for the entire Whidbey Island area. During the Kennedy Administration, the tunnels were well stocked with food, water, medicine and detection equipment, but the lack of supervision and local support made most of these efforts and the work of Roy Evans as futile as the fund-raising dance. Vandals continually broke into the headquarters building to steal the drugs and quite a bit of the supplies spoiled with age. As Roy Evans admitted,

> *We had a constant problem with vandalism especially when the Seattle newspapers would announce what medical supplies were in the bunkers. Every time the supplies were listed in the papers, every drug addict in the area would head for the fort, break the locks off and take everything. They just took the drugs not the food. Apparently survival biscuits weren't in big demand.*[12]

The whole concept of volunteers, living miles away in Oak Harbor and Coupeville, leaving their families and making their way to the fort in the event of a nuclear emergency to unlock doors and open tunnels, was extremely naive. Evans also laughed at the Federal government trying to convince the CD County Directors that people wouldn't mind being in those tunnels if an atomic bomb was dropped.

> *What real good would Casey have been in the event of an atomic attack? To begin with there was only one real road to the fort and that was supposed to service the entire island. What would you do if a truck blocked Deception Pass Bridge? Then there were the tunnels themselves. They weren't ventilated anywhere near properly, there were no lights or electricity, there were no bathrooms, and the nearest running water was a quarter of a mile away. They even did a survey of the fort and estimated that 5,000 people could survive in there, standing nose to nose maybe. They were just for blast protection and really just lip service for a program that was never properly supported ideologically or financially.*[13]

While Roy Evans and Civil Defense struggled with their problems, the State Parks, which now owned the upper portion of Casey, were slowly proceeding with their plans to restore the fort. It had been decided to return the historic site to as close to its original condition as possible. The Admiralty Head Lighthouse was being restored and an interpretive museum was to be built inside. Railings and walkways, which had been removed during World War II, had to be reinstalled, and a number of the tunnels were permanently sealed for public safety.

John Vanderzicht, who was now the director of the State Parks, was instrumental in the restoration, yet even in the process a major ingredient was missing: the guns. Because of the massive scrap metal drive that had swept through Puget Sound and the rest of the country in 1942, there were very few weapons of the 1890-1910 Endicott Period left in existence. In fact, to this day, there are more examples of Civil War artillery preserved in the nation than of the World War I-II periods.[14] To the State Parks and those involved with the restoration at Admiralty Head, their work would not be complete until some examples of the type of weapons used could also be restored. Unfortunately, there just were none left in the United States.

The hunt for Endicott-type weapons continued. In late 1960, the search was rewarded with news of a find in the jungles of the Philippines. Two different people are credited with discovering the guns that sat rusting and forgotten at Fort Wint on Grande Island in Subic Bay. One source points to a sailor

ABOVE: Many felt the restoration of Fort Casey would never be complete without examples of the main weapons that helped protect the Northwest. Unfortunately, the only examples of these turn-of-the-century weapons left in the world were located at Fort Wint in the Philippines. The weapons had been abandoned since the end of World War I and bringing them to Washington would require a herculean effort on the part of the State Parks, State Government, and local civic groups.

RIGHT: US Navy personnel stationed near Fort Wint volunteered to help disassemble the rifles and their carriages for transport back to Washington. This required weeks of back breaking work in tropical heat to break 20 years of rust and abandonment. None of the men involved had ever heard of Fort Casey before.

stationed at Subic Bay, John Van Dyke, as the first to send word back to the Coupeville area. Van Dyke, who had been stationed at the Whidbey Naval Air Station, contacted life-long Coupeville resident Mickey Clark and sent pictures of the weapons where they rested in their original emplacements. Grande Island, where Fort Wint is located, had been converted into a rest and recreation site for U. S. Navy personnel on leave from active duty in Viet Nam. Van Dyke contacted Clark and even sent an article about the guns that had been printed in the *Whidbey News Times*.

> *Even though they haven't fired a shot since early in World War II and probably have been abandoned for about three-fourths of that time, they are in remarkably good condition. They show obvious signs of having suffered through a terrific battle, such as deep pock marks on the barrels and associated machinery. These scars are reminders that the Japanese were driven out of this area and sought refuge in the casements and connecting tunnels of this battery. Before the Japanese gave up this installation they were determined that little that they were forced to abandon could be of any use to their enemies. After their recapture by American forces the guns were no longer useful against modern fighting technology so they were simply abandoned. Here sat the sentinels of the past forgotten by most but protected by foliage of a creeping jungle.*[15]

Apparently, not much more happened after he made his discovery and alerted his friend in Coupeville.

The second individual who is more widely acknowledged as the finder of the forgotten guns is Lieutenant Commander David Kirschner. Also having been stationed at Whidbey, Kirschner, who was a member of the Cannon Hunters Association of Seattle (CHAOS), learned of the search for the guns while on duty in the Philippines. As a pilot, he did a great deal of flying over the jungle-covered islands of the area and is said to have initially spotted the old guns shining in the sun one day while on a flight over one of the pre-World War I coastal defense forts. He later investigated on foot and discovered the long untouched 10-inch and 3-inch guns still emplaced where they had been left at the end of World War II. He notified local officials and the State Parks Department, which expressed interest in acquiring the guns and bringing them back to Washington.

For the State of Washington to take possession of those guns, the first order of business was to negotiate with the Philippine government, an independent nation since 1946, which now legally owned them. When permission to take the guns was granted the next step was to have the Navy Department declare them surplus, since they were still considered potential weapons. This was done in March of 1961. The next step was to arrange for the dismantling of the guns and their transportation to Seattle. This turned out to be the biggest problem of them all.

In August of 1962, it was announced that Fort Casey would be officially dedicated as an historic site. With the guns transferred from Fort Wint and the progress of the restoration, it was an appropriate time to finally recognize the historic value of the fort. On Sunday, September 9, 1962, dignitaries and the public gathered at Admiralty Head for the official ceremony. Retired General Edward C. Dohm, National Guard Coast Artillery, and State Parks Commissioner John Vanderzicht each spoke briefly and Fort Casey was dedicated. The land that had once been Dr. John Kellogg's pasture was officially recognized for the part it had played in the defense of the nation through two world wars.

While this was going on at Admiralty Head, the Navy was wrestling with the job of dismantling

ABOVE: US Navy personnel loading one of the four salvaged 3" guns onto a ship for transport to Subic Bay. Two would be remounted at Fort Flagler and two at Battery Trevor at Fort Casey.

RIGHT: On May 7, 1963 the first of Fort Casey's guns returned with the mounting of two three-inch rapid fire rifles at Battery Trevor. Though not the original weapons, these similar guns were brought from Fort Wint in the Philippines and were mounted by the U. S. Navy which provided the crane. Amazingly the guns fit into the emplacements mounts perfectly.

the guns and transporting them from Fort Wint to Seattle. The question now was where the money would come from to pay for it all. The preliminary cost estimates for dismantling and shipping two 10-inch disappearing guns and their carriages and four 3-inch pedestal mounted guns, came in at about $10,000. The state budgeted money for this, but was a little upset when a re-evaluation of the project by the Navy raised the cost to over $30,000. The study indicated it would take that much to build roads and raise power lines in the area just to get the huge guns to the dock. The seventeen years of neglect since WW II had allowed the jungle to completely overgrow the original roads and the fort. Also, the guns themselves were completely rusted over. By all accounts they were in a remarkable state of preservation considering the fighting that had taken place in the area, but they still had been exposed to the elements and jungle for close to a quarter century. This was far more money than the State Parks had or could afford, so it was decided to just bring the smaller 3-inch guns, which were more accessible, to Washington first. This was accomplished by May 6, 1963.[16]

Again with the aid of the Navy, two 3-inch guns were mounted at Fort Flagler and two were installed in Battery Trevor at Fort Casey. The *Whidbey News-Times* reported:

'Installation of two 3-inch cannon at Fort Casey State Historical Site Monday marked an important part in the restoration of the fort, Dick Clifton, Head of the State parks and Recreation Department said. 'We asked the Navy to provide a crane to lift the six-ton, 12 ½ foot rifle barrels into position in the gun emplacements. The guns, scarred by strafing, possibly from American planes in the recapturing of Fort Wint, PI, fitted directly on the mounts in the 3-inch battery and were installed with the help of a Navy crane in less than an hour. The rapid fire weapons are just like those which were located at Casey from the turn of the century until after World War II.'[17]

Work now began on raising the money to get the two 10-inch guns to Casey. This would prove to be a long and difficult process. A number of local civic organizations took part in fund-raising drives, but it was principally the work of the Coupeville Lions Club and one of its members, Wilber Sherman, that was the motivating force in raising the money. In 1965 the club launched a "Guns for Coupeville" campaign and for approximately the next five years worked to raise money. Other groups helped at one time or another, as did various local political representatives, to support the Lions Club drive.

There was also a great deal of support from high-ranking officials. In October of 1965, the Governor of the State of Washington, Daniel J. Evans, signed a proclamation designating November as "Guns for Fort Casey" month.

In this changing world we are too often prone to forget the importance of keeping from oblivion the few remnants of our past, as in the case of Fort Casey.

Now, therefore, I, Daniel J. Evans, Governor of the State of Washington, do hereby designate the period of the entire month of November, 1965, as: GUNS FOR FORT CASEY MONTH in the state of Washington.[18]

The support of Senator Henry Jackson was also vital in securing the guns. At the time, there were other parties who were also interested in obtaining the guns. The Smithsonian Institute was very

ABOVE: The Sea-land Company volunteered to transport the two guns and their carriages back to Seattle from the Philippines. During the voyage the container ship was pummeled by a fierce Pacific storm and one of the 35 ton barrels broke loose. The railing on the deck is all that kept the barrel from going overboard and being lost forever. This is the sight that greeted the State Parks Director as the ship was docked at Harbor Island in Seattle.

RIGHT: One of the two 35 ton gun tubes is lowered onto the lowboy trailer for transportation to Bremerton Naval Shipyard for restoration.

anxious to get the weapons, as was the State of Oregon. Because of the thoroughness of the WW II scrap drives, the two 10-inch rifles at Fort Wint were the only remaining examples of that type of artillery left in the world. The other guns remaining at Wint were in no condition to be salvaged, so these were the last ones to be had. If Casey wanted to get the two guns, they would have to pull out all the stops, both financially and politically. No stone was left unturned to raise money and support.[19]

Finally by 1968, the needed funds had been raised to bring the last two remaining 10-inch disappearing guns from the Philippines to Washington. It took over $1,700 from the Coupeville Lions Club, $2,500 from the American Legion Post in Oak Harbor and a special appropriation by the 1967 State Legislature of $31,000 to pay the cost of dismantling and transporting to the Subic Bay docks. As before, the Navy was assigned the task, but for many who took part, it was work they did voluntarily. Navy Lieutenant Gerald R. Stott was the supervisor of the back-breaking job of taking the guns apart.

> *The work of dismantling the guns has fallen into four stages. Last November we began putting penetrating oil into anything that had to be disassembled. It is used to break the bonds of rust between two metal surfaces, such as nuts, bolts, or frozen bearings. Late in December we started stripping the catwalks and stagings and lowering the guns from the elevated firing position to the loading position. Two men then spent an entire week with sledge hammers breaking the rust seal on nuts and bolts that held many of the pieces of the guns together. When this was done we were able to proceed with the disassembling of the weapons and preparing them for shipment back to Seattle. The crew worked 12 hours a day, seven days a week to get the project done on time and within the allotted budget.*
>
> *Cobras and other deadly poisonous snakes are often found in and around the old battery but the crew, at some risk to themselves, examined the site thoroughly and found parts which had not seen daylight for 25 years.*
>
> *Local rumor had it that the breech blocks, which were removed before the Japanese captured the fort, were in the counterweight well beneath the guns. Unfortunately, because of the snake danger none of the local workers would go down into the wells. The sailors crawled down the 25 foot well shaft into two feet of mud. They did not find the blocks, but they did bring up some bearing caps.*
>
> *None of the men working on the project are from Washington but they all say they will make a special trip to see the guns when they are restored.*[20]

Once the Navy had moved the 250 tons of guns and carriages to the Subic Bay docks, they were loaded on board the Sea-Land container ship *San Francisco* bound for Seattle. The transportation from the Philippines was provided free by Sea-Land but not necessarily without risk. Because of their size, the gun tubes and their carriages had to be secured on the upper deck. During the voyage, a storm was encountered that was violent enough to cause one of the 10-inch gun tubes to break loose from its moorings. Considerable damage was done to the Sea-Land ship by the rolling 35+ ton barrel and when some of the lead counterweights also broke loose and fell through the decking, there was a very real danger to the container ship. Had the tube completely broken free, in all probability, it would have gone overboard and been lost forever. By a stroke of amazing luck one of the two collar studs at the end of the barrel caught on the deck railing during the storm and this gave crewmen on the ship

ABOVE: Once the guns were unloaded they were taken to the Bremerton Naval Shipyards for restoration. The weapons and their carriages were sandblasted and painted before they were transported to Fort Casey for installation.

RIGHT: Like the 3-inch rifles installed in 1963, the base rings and the carriages from the Philippines fit nearly perfectly into the Battery Worth emplacements at Fort Casey. Some alterations had to be made due to war damage and the addition of ladders and walkways for public use. The U. S. Navy again provided cranes to help in lifting the heavy carriage parts while volunteer workers from the Naval Shipyard performed the installation.

time to chain the gun tube down until the storm abated. Once the weather improved, the barrel was refastened and the ship and cargo arrived safely in Seattle.

Jim Collins was the head ranger at Fort Casey during this time and was present with other state officials at Harbor Island in Seattle when the *San Francisco* finally docked.

> *It was pretty amazing to see that gun barrel protruding over the side of the ship as it was docked. Each barrel has two collar studs that are near the rear of the tube. It was one of these that caught on the deck railing and kept it from going overboard during the storm. That stud was all that kept it from being lost. Sea Land ate the cost of the damage and were very anxious, to say the least, to get the guns off their ship.*[21]

Once safely docked, the gun tubes could now be unloaded and sent to the Puget Sound Naval Shipyard at Bremerton for restoration. The Navy had sent one of its biggest cranes from Bremerton to help with the unloading. Again, this involved some tense moments. While one of the tubes was being lowered from the ship, it partially broke free from its lines and almost crashed through the dock. State parks officials must have breathed a huge sigh of relief when the guns were finally safely on the ground and on their way to Bremerton.[22]

At Bremerton the guns and their carriages were sand blasted and then painted with a primer coat to weatherize them as much as possible from the salt air. While this was going on, a road was bulldozed from the main road into the park to the front of Battery Worth where the guns would be mounted.

Once the restoration of the guns and their carriages was complete they were transported by lowboy trailers to Fort Casey where they would be mounted in emplacements Number 1 and Number 2 of Battery William Worth. Again some problems arose as Ranger Collins described:

> *Moving these huge barrels, their carriages, the railings, and the counterweights was a very slow and difficult process. Moving over 250+ tons of metal by trailer required a bit more planning than was expected. The only way to get to Casey by road required taking a ferry from Port Townsend. One of the trailers carrying a gun tube became stuck while being unloaded at the Keystone Ferry dock. While bringing it off the ferry it was discovered that the tide was too low and due to the huge weight of the gun the trailer became wedged between the dock and the ferry deck. They had to wait for the tide to come in to raise the ferry up and it closed down the ferry for one complete run before they could get it off.*[23]

Hopefully everyone else on board the ferry had been allowed to off load their cars before the trailer became stuck.

Once the guns and their carriages arrived at Fort Casey the job of remounting these salvaged weapons began. All the work at Bremerton and at Casey was performed by Naval Shipyard workers. They volunteered to come to the fort to do the work but were paid by the shipyard. They brought their wives and lived in campers and trailers behind the main emplacements while the work was going on. Most of the men had never been to Fort Casey but like the Navy men who labored so hard in the Philippines they said they truly enjoyed doing the work. They were restoring history and helping to preserve part of our national heritage.[24]

The job of remounting these turn-of-the-century weapons must have seemed a daunting one to the shipyard workers, none of whom had ever seen weapons like these before. The gun pits at Battery Worth had to first be cleaned and the site prepped to allow access as the jigsaw puzzle of pieces, some weighing many tones, were spread out in the field adjacent to the emplacements . The Navy brought in two large cranes to begin lifting the parts into place, piece by piece. Amazingly the carriage rings fit perfectly when placed on the old fittings. The counterbalances, however, were not the same. The United States Army design for coast artillery emplacements was fairly standard throughout the world. The only differences were due to the geography of the land where the fortifications were constructed. The guns from the Philippines were close but not the same as the original weapons. This meant that the workers had to modify and in some cases prefabricate things to fit. The original Battery Worth disappearing rifles had lead counterweights to raise the guns for firing. The ones from the Philippines were cast iron. This required some modifications in installation. Ranger Jim Collins joked:

> *Because the counterweights were different, a number of the cast iron weights from the Philippines models had to be left off. Even if the guns were workable there was not enough weight on these counterweights to raise the guns. Despite the wishful thinking of some of the old vets who showed up to watch, these guns were not going to ever fire again.*[25]

There were also a number of parts on the carriages that had been destroyed during the war. Again this required the shipyard workers to be creative in assembling the carriages, building new steps and platforms, and in general making them safe for the public which would soon be climbing all over them.

As the carriages were assembled in the pits, new problems arose due to the massive weights involved. Because of the geography of the emplacements the most practical way of lifting parts and delivering them to the workers was from above on the bluff, then loading downward. The cranes were positioned above the parapets and would lower parts down into the pits with the wheels of the equipment right at the edge of the concrete walls. The cranes the Navy sent for mounting the guns were not as large as they wanted and on a couple of occasions things got pretty tense because they were lifting right at their load limits. In one instance, while raising a large piece of one of the carriages, the wood bracing just crumbled during the lift and there was a real chance of the crane being pulled over into the pit. Ranger Collins recalled,

> *We knew things were getting a little tense when they ordered everyone off the emplacements and asked all the observers to go out into the field away from Battery Worth. Luckily they were able to reinforce the wood cribbing and the lift was safely completed.*[26]

When it came time to place one of the 35 ton gun tubes into place two cranes were employed and even then the length of the barrel presented lifting problems. It is interesting to note that when the fort was in its younger days, each of the 10-inch rifle barrels was removed and the carriages disassembled once a year for cleaning and maintenance. This yearly task was performed using blocks and tackles, large timbers, and Army mule power. The large steel rings located on the emplacement walls of each of the battery pits were specifically used for this purpose. Looking much like large door knockers, these rings were part of the design that enabled the soldiers to run ropes and support lines that were part of the process used to remove the gun barrels and carriages. Corps of Engineer records show that the gun crews were capable of assembling or disassembling a 10-inch rifle in a couple of days. This was all done by hand as cranes were not available at the fort. What was now taking weeks and involving some tense moments with diesel powered cranes, was once done by enlisted men and four legged horse power.

It was decided to place one of the guns in the raised or firing position and the other in the down or loading position. Unfortunately, one of the last pieces needed to complete the guns restoration was not available. The breech blocks, those essential locking mechanisms located at the butt end of every rear end loading weapon, did not make the trip from the Philippines. There were conflicting reports as to what happened to them. One story said they were thrown into Subic Bay by the Americans as the Japanese took control of Grande Island where Fort Wint was located. Though obsolete and damaged in the battle for the island, the American troops didn't want to take any chances that the enemy would ever get the guns working again. Another story stated the Japanese threw the blocks into the bay to keep the Americans from possibly restoring the guns. Whatever actually happened to the blocks has been lost in the confusion of the fighting over 60 years ago. Whatever the reasons none were found by the Marines at Fort Wint and they were not something that could be made from scrap by the Bremerton Shipyard workers.

Finally, on Sunday, August 11, 1968, over seven years after the first steps were made to procure them, the last two remaining 10-inch disappearing rifles were dedicated at Fort Casey State Park. The ceremony was attended by Senator Henry M. Jackson, Governor Daniel J. Evans, and local dignitaries from around the area. The Washington National Guard Band played, speeches were made and the memory of the men who served their nation was remembered. Fort Casey now received more recognition in retirement than it had ever achieved in over 50 years of service. A large bronze plaque was placed on the side of one of the concrete walls at Battery Worth commemorating Fort Casey and the work done by so many to bring the guns to Admiralty Head. The fort and its weapons of war had now come full circle. What was once meant to project destruction would now provide hundreds of thousands with enjoyment and excitement. The tunnels that had once housed tons of explosives were now dark, mysterious places just waiting for the joyous screams of inquisitive little children. Where mid-west farmers-turned-soldiers had once trained for war, school children would now learn something of the history of their nation. Fort Casey was, and still is serving the people of Coupeville and Washington.

In November of 1966, the Washington State Parks Department enlarged Fort Casey State Park with the leasing of 27.6 more acres of land. Most of this was by the Ferry Landing and would be used for public camp sites. The land was leased from the Department of the Army for $1.00 on a ten year basis and was renewed in 1976. The land had been part of the original John C. Kellogg Donation Land Claim made before the turn of the century. This brought the total area of the State Park to 137.6 acres.[27]

There have been other changes at Fort Casey since the dedication of the guns in 1968. Little by little, time continues to eat away at the buildings and the emplacements. A few more of the original buildings have been removed because of collapse or as potential hazards, most notably, the Fire Control Station near the lighthouse. A heavy snowfall in September of 1968 caved in the building that at one

LEFT: Two of the Navy's cranes were required to lower the 35 ton barrel into place and even that strained their lifting power to the limit. Notice there are no workers anywhere near the gun carriage or in the immediate vicinity on the parapet as the barrel is lowered into place.

BELOW: Workers apply the final weatherizing coat of paint to the guns and their carriages. This 10-inch rifle is in the down or loading position where it was invisible to ships out in Admiralty Inlet thus its name a disappearing rifle. The other gun on the right is in the firing position. Note the large black rings on the walls of the emplacement. They were used by the troops at the turn of the century to install and remove the gun tubes and carriages for yearly maintenance. All of their work was done using ropes, pulleys, and man power.

time directed the fire of all the guns at Casey; also removed after the snowfall was the converted radio shack opposite the Switchboard. In the years that followed, the NCO Club, above the dock area, was removed, as were the plotting rooms at the mortars. In 1979, a change was made in the Corps of Engineers' lease at the Ferry slip. Additional land was needed to meet increased parking needs for ferry traffic. The original .83 acres was increased to 1.14 acres and improvements to the dock, the harbor basin and the access area were made.[28]

As late as September, 1969, however, agreements were still in use designating the tunnels of Batteries Moore, Kingsbury, Worth, and the Central Power Plant as viable shelter facilities. It was projected that over 1,000 people could be temporarily sheltered in these emplacements. Fortunately, they were never needed. The use of the tunnels for Civil Defense shelters finally was abandoned in 1972. All of the signs were removed and many of the bunkers were welded permanently shut. The supplies that had been stored in them were removed and for the most part thrown out. The silliness of the whole concept of using the 70-year-old tunnels for protection from fallout was at last realized, although as late as 1974 they were still considered usable. A few of the smaller rooms at Battery Trevor and Van Horne were kept locked for possible use in the future and, in fact, were opened for public use in 1979.

In July, the Department of Emergency Services announced to the general public in the Coupeville-Oak Harbor vicinity that shelter was available for those fearing the fall of Skylab. Since the path of the returning space station passed over Whidbey Island, it was a matter of preparedness to have the area's only large public shelters open for anyone who wished to use them. No one did.

Today, Fort Casey exists as one of the major tourist attractions in the state. Camping facilities near the Keystone Ferry dock and a newly opened section on the Seattle Pacific portion of the old reservation are used throughout the year by thousands. Well over 400,000 people a year visit or camp at Admiralty Head. School children from all over the area annually visit the fort and marvel at the construction and sheer size of the guns. The lighthouse, saved by the Washington State Parks in the mid-1950s, is still open to the public but now under the direction of the Washington State University Extension program. In the early 1990s funding cutbacks, a continual problem for the State Parks, led to the loss of the lighthouse's interpretive ranger. In 1994, an agreement was reached with the Washington State University Environmental Program to keep the lighthouse open to the public in exchange for much needed office space in the lighthouse. Today WSU manages the Interpretive Center including the Beachwatchers Program and Environmental Program, out of the lighthouse. The lighthouse celebrated its Centennial in 2003. As a part of the Ebey's Landing National Historic Reserve the restoration of other portions of Fort Casey and a number of its original structures continues. Plans have been made to reconstruct the Fire Commander's Station in its original location and efforts are being made to restore the park's cultural landscape.

It is, however, unfortunate that so much of the original railings, ladders, guns, and equipment have been lost to scrap drives and the elements over the years. With each loss, a little bit of history vanishes. The State Parks Department has done a remarkable job in restoring Casey, but they are fighting a losing battle. Each day, the salt air eats away a little more at the concrete and crumbles a little more from the bluff beneath the searchlights. The observation posts that provided target information are, one by one, being removed. Public misuse has led to the sealing up and, in some cases, removal of certain structures. Bit by bit, time is taking its toll.

Fort Casey is a relic. Its impressive walls of earth and stone are no longer important from a military standpoint. The huge guns that once protected Seattle and Bremerton have been replaced by satellites, missiles, and the jet. What was originally built to guard and defend has now become a peaceful tourist attraction. Seacoast defense is now no longer possible, but for over 150 years this nation depended upon it for protection. Coast defense was considered a prime necessity from the days of George Washington to those of George Marshall. It was a true reflection of the American attitude in an age that hoped for a peaceful aloofness from the rest of the world yet was determined to defend itself from any possible foreign attack.[29]

With each passing day, the world moves further and further away from Fort Casey and the reasons for which it was built. Yet people from all walks of life continually come to see and be impressed by it. It is hard to not be impressed by the engineering skill and craftsmanship that went into the fort and its weapons. Fort Casey is from another era. Those who designed, built, and first served there are all gone, but their legacy is carried on by what remains. A feeling of history lingers throughout the tunnels and passageways at Admiralty Head. It is a sense of having made contact with a tangible substance of the past. No matter how many buildings are removed, no matter how many cracks appear in the concrete walls, it will survive. It will live on in the memories of those surviving veterans who served at Admiralty Head in times of peace and war. Though Casey's weapons never fired a shot in anger nor played a major part in the history of our country, it did serve a vital function. It was part of a national system of defense that protected our freedom for over 40 years. It remains the silent sentinel, facing the waters of Admiralty Inlet and her sister forts of the old Harbor Defense.

EPILOGUE

I HAVE VISITED FORT CASEY MORE TIMES THAN I WOULD VENTURE TO GUESS. SOME WERE FOR THE pleasure of just exploring, some were to gather information, and some were to share. Much like a mirror reflecting the stages of my life, my experiences have grown and changed through the years. I ran joyously from place to place as a youth, sought hidden secrets and answers as a researching student, and then tried to educate and inform others who asked many of the same questions I once did. Unlike the casual weekend visitor, it is difficult to see and appreciate this historic landmark in one or two short hours. Watching people fly kites from the top of the bluff or families picnic in the field behind the main emplacement are common sites, but too often I envision something totally different. My mind sees soldiers pushing shot carts across the parapets, elevators bringing up powder bags from the magazines below, or the sound of a window rattling boom as one of the huge rifles spit out its shell toward a distant target in the Inlet.

The books I have read, the hundreds of graphic images and photographs I have collected, and the interviews all have brought Fort Casey to life. They are vivid memories that will always be there to remind me of this monument to our nation's history, but there will always be something else, something special that still sends that little chill up my spine each time I drive on the road past the Ranger's home and see those massive walls, darkened doorways, and stark concrete towers.

I was 14 years old in 1962 when on a Sunday drive we somehow ended up at Fort Casey. My family had only moved to Oak Harbor a couple of months earlier and we were out exploring the area. My father was renowned for locating out-of-the-way unusual places that never really interested my mother or me on these weekend excursions. This turned out to not be one of those occasions. To me this particular Sunday was one of those rare, life-altering moments. Following the tree-lined, main road past the picnic area and the Ranger's home, we emerged into the bright sunlight and the main emplacements were revealed in all their glory. Pulling into a gravel parking area my father stopped the car, turned and asked me if I wanted to get out and "look around." Two hours later he was

LEFT: My first picture with a trusty Instamatic camera. This is at Battery Valleau in 1969. The fort was still pretty open and in places dangerous as the open counterweight well shows. That is the Keystone-Port Townsend ferry in the background. Including it in the shot was unintentional as was the photographer's image.

OPPOSITE PAGE: Fort Casey today - main emplacements.

RIGHT: One of two searchlight emplacements located on the bluff in front of the main batteries. Weather and erosion have gradually eaten away the bluff until the emplacement is no longer safe for public use. It seems only a matter of time before this structure, like many other coast artillery positions will have to be removed.

honking the car horn trying to get me to come back so we could go home. Fort Casey had its hooks in me and I have been looking around ever since.

As I grew, so did my interest in the fort and everything about it. This would take me into every museum and historical society in the area, interviews with every surviving veteran that I could locate, and hours of conversations with local residents in the Coupeville/Whidbey Island area. I traveled across the country to the National Archives in Washington D. C. to pour through mountains of files from the Corps of Engineers and to the Library of Congress to view military records. My devotion to this topic led me to a degree in History and eventually a Master's with this as my Magnum Opus. I chose education as my profession and 34 years spent teaching elementary students, but no matter what the student age, Fort Casey always managed to be involved. I truly believe that you need to know the history of your community and state to appreciate where you live. This philosophy of history took my class of students to Admiralty Head for an all day field trip 29 of those 34 years. Each time the bus would drive past that Ranger's house and we would see the sweeping view of those concrete walls and massive guns, I would relive the moment with my students as I had in 1962. Watching their looks of wonder and amazement always brought back all the same feelings I had on that Sunday afternoon. What had changed was that now I was honking the horn and trying my best to control that wondrous enthusiasm as we walked and talked the history of the fort.

There are times when history is boring and void of relevance to children or adults. Not so at Fort Casey. When you can climb the same ladders that soldiers did in 1901, can touch guns that actually fought to protect our nation, and walk the dark tunnels that hundreds of servicemen walked in their daily job of defending our freedom, it becomes real. While walking the parapets of a gun emplacement this history is not an abstraction but a tangible reality that millions of visitors have had the opportunity to experience. The work being done by the Washington State Parks and the various historic organizations to preserve and restore the fort are more than laudable, they are necessary. Preserving the past can give us insights into our present day circumstances and help us to visualize our future. Fort Casey is a link to that past, a past that needs to be honored and remembered.

LEFT: A view of one of the two pits at Battery Schenck. The holes for two of the 12-inch mortars are visible at the bottom. The doorways lead into the ammunition tunnel that circles the pit. The fire control blockhouse is at the top of the picture. This is where the Civil Defense was prepared to have people go to wait out a nuclear attack.

RIGHT: A closer view of one of the mortar blockhouses. The metal railing on the side are where fire directions were communicated to the gun crews. Messages were received via telephone, instructions were written in chalk on slate panels and then were slid out on the railings for the gun crews to read. They were slid back in and remarked as new fire coordinates were received.

ABOVE, BELOW: The Fort Wint guns were installed at Fort Casey by 1968. The netting was added as were additional ladders for public safety. The weapons are impressive in their own right but seeing the battle scars which cover the guns and carriages adds to the historic character of the monuments.

APPENDIX A

FORT CASEY GUN BATTERY HISTORIES

BATTERY KINGSBURY

Named for Colonel Henry Kingsbury, 11th Connecticut Volunteers. Upon graduation from West Point he was appointed second lieutenant of ordnance, May 4, 1861. He took part in the Manassas campaign and the Battle of Bull Run, serving as aide to General McDowell. In command of his regiment, the 11th Connecticut, during the Maryland campaign of 1862, he led the attack in Burnside's Corps against the Confederates at Burnside Bridge, where he was mortally wounded. He died September 18, 1862.

Two 10-inch rifles mounted on disappearing carriages. The emplacements were built between March 1901 and June 1904 at a cost of $92,261.60. Power supply was from power plant at #3 Battery Moore or from commercial sources. Data transmission was by telephone. Guns No. 1 & 2 turned over to Artillery November 27, 1905. Gun tube of gun No. 1 taken down in 1909 and was to be stored locally for use as a spare in the Ninth Corps Area. The carriage was to be sold as scrap but was later retained for parts and maintenance. In actuality the gun tube was stored on the ground in the vicinity of the battery and the carriage was left in place. The gun was remounted in September 1920. Gun No. 2 was removed June 7, 1918 and its carriage was salvaged September 28, 1920. Gun No. 1 was declared "No longer required" on February 23, 1933. The gun was declared obsolete armament during the "Salvage of Obsolete Armament" movement and was cut up for scrap and removed October 24, 1942.

BATTERY MOORE

Named for Brigadier General James Moore, Continental Army. Of high political standing in his native state of North Carolina, he was appointed colonel 1st North Carolina Militia, September 1, 1775. On March 1 of the following year he was advanced to the rank of brigadier general Continental Army. His activities were confined to operations in the South; his most notable success was at Moore's Crossing where, on February 27, 1776, he defeated and captured a large force of Scotch Royalists. This action advanced the cause of independence. The British dropped their plans for conquering the Southern colonies and postponed their major moves in the South until later in the war. Moore died April 9, 1777.

Three 10-inch rifles mounted on disappearing carriages: The emplacements were built between September 1897 and June 1902 at a cost of $98,078. Guns # 1 and #2 were completed by 1899 but gun #3 was not finished until 1904 because of problems with bluff erosion at the end of the emplacement foundation. Guns #1 & 2 were turned over to the Artillery on June 16, 1902, and gun #3 on November 27, 1905. Data transmission was my telephone. Power supply was from power plant at #3 Battery Moore or from commercial sources. Guns and carriages were declared "no longer required" on February 23, 1933. The guns were declared obsolete armament during the "Salvage of Obsolete Armament" movement and were cut up for scrap and removed October 24, 1942.

BATTERY PARKER

The battery was named in honor of Brevet First Lieutenant Thomas D. Parker, 2nd Infantry. Parker enlisted in the Army on January 6, 1860, and served in the ranks as a noncommissioned officer until he was commissioned second lieutenant, 2nd Infantry, October 24, 1861. He took part in the Peninsular Campaign and while leading a charge of his regiment at the Battle of Gaines Mill, Virginia, he was instantly killed, June 17, 1862. It was for his courageous action on this occasion that the brevetcy was awarded posthumously.

Two 6-inch rifles mounted on disappearing carriages: The emplacements were built between August 1903 and August 1905 at a cost of $50,380. The power supply was from the mortar power station or commercial sources. Data transmission was by telephone. It was turned over to Artillery May 22, 1907. Gun tubes were removed November 21, 1917 and were shipped to the Watervliet Arsenal, New York. The carriages were cut up and sold for scrap September 30, 1920.

BATTERY SCHENCK

Named for Lieutenant Colonel Alexander Dubois Schenck, Artillery Corps. He enlisted in the 1st Ohio Infantry, April 17, 1861. During his enlisted service he took part in the battles of Bull Run, Perryville, Stone River, and Hoover's Gap. Graduating from West Point June 17, 1867, he was commissioned second lieutenant, 2nd Infantry, and advanced to the rank of lieutenant colonel. He died September 16, 1905.

Eight 12-inch mortars: The emplacements were built between March 1898 and the end of 1899 at a cost of $46,603. The power supply was from the mortar power station or commercial sources. Data transmission was by telephone. It was turned over to Artillery on June 16, 1902. In 1940 the guns were declared outmoded during the Modernization of Harbor Defense Project, Continental United States. The guns were declared obsolete armament during the 'Salvage of Obsolete Armament' movement and were cut up for scrap and removed October 24, 1942.

BATTERY SEYMOUR

Named for Major Truman Seymour, 6th U.S. Artillery, and brevet major general, U.S. Army. He graduated from West Point, July 1, 1845. In the Mexican War he was brevetted first lieutenant and captain in 1847 for gallant conduct in the battles of Cerro Gordo, Centraras, and Cherubusco. He too part in the Florida hostilities against the Seminoles, 1856-1858. At the outbreak of the Civil War he commanded his battery in defense of Fort Sumter. He was brevetted major April 24, 1861, lieutenant colonel September 14, 1862, and colonel September 17, 1862 for gallant and meritorious service.

Eight 12-inch mortars: The emplacement was built between March 1898 and the end of 1899 at a cost of $46,603. It was turned over to Artillery June 16, 1902. The power supply was from the mortar power station or commercial sources. Data transmission was by telephone. The two forward guns in each of the two pits were removed May 24, 1918, and shipped to I. O. Morgan Engineering Works, Alliance, Ohio. Their carriages were cut up for scrap and removed December 9, 1920. The remaining two guns in each pit were declared outmoded in 1940. In 1940 the guns were declared outmoded during the Modernization of Harbor Defense Project, Continental United States. The guns were declared obsolete armament during the "Salvage of Obsolete Armament" movement and were cut up for scrap and removed October 24, 1942.

BATTERY TREVOR

Named for First Lieutenant John Trevor, 5th Cavalry. Enlisted in the Army during 1858, he served in Battery C, 5th Artillery until 1864, when he was appointed second lieutenant, 5th Cavalry. He served with Merritt's Division, Sheridan's Army, in the Shenandoah Valley. He was fatally wounded in the Battle of Winchester, Virginia, September 19, 1864.

Two 3-inch rapid fire rifles on barbette mounts: The emplacement was built between August 1903 and June 1905 at a cost of $15,800. Data transmission was by telephone. Power supply was from power station at #3 Battery Moore. It was turned over to Artillery May 22, 1907. Gun tubes were removed on November 2, 1933 and were shipped to Fort Mills, In the Philippines. The carriages were authorized for salvage in the "Salvage of Obsolete Armament" movement and cut up for scrap and removed October 24, 1942.

BATTERY TURMAN

Named for Second Lieutenant Reuben Smith Turman, 5th Infantry. He enlisted in the Army in May of 1893, was appointed second lieutenant March 23, 1896, and was assigned to the 5th Infantry. While taking part in the engagement at San Juan Hill, Cuba, July 1, 1898, he was mortally wounded, and died three days later.

Two 5-inch rapid fire rifles mounted on balanced pillars: the emplacement was built between June 1899 and June 1902 at a cost of $18,850. Data transmission was by telephone. Power was from station #3 Battery Moore or from commercial sources. It was turned over to Artillery on June 16, 1902 but the gun tubes were not installed until mid-1903. The guns tubes were removed on May 21, 1918, and shipped to Sandy Hook Proving Grounds, Sandy Hook, New Jersey. The carriages were scrapped by September 29, 1920.

BATTERY VALLEAU

Named for First Lieutenant John Valleau, 13th Infantry, appointed March 24, 1812. On October 12 of the same year, his company formed part of the force assembled at Lewiston for an attack on Queenston Heights. He was with the first troops to land on the Canadian side. On the following day he was killed in the first assault.

Four 6-inch rifles mounted on disappearing carriages: The emplacement was built between October 1903 and March 1907 at a cost of $92,125. Power source was from #3 Battery Moore engine room, the Central power plant or commercial sources. Data transmission was by telephone. It was turned over to Artillery May 22, 1907 but the gun tubes weren't installed until August 5, 1908. The gun tubes removed by November 9, 1919 and were shipped to Watervliet Arsenal, New York. The carriages were cut up and sold for scrap September 21, 1920.

BATTERY VAN HORNE

Named for Captain Issac Van Horne, Jr., 19th U.S. Infantry. Appointed captain 27th U. S. Infantry, May 20, 1813; transferred to the 19th Infantry a year later. He took part in a number of expeditions under Colonel Croghan against Fort Mackinac. He was killed in the attack on that point August 4, 1814.

Two 3-inch rapid fire rifles on barbette mounts: The emplacement was built between August 1903 and June 1905 at a cost of $15,800. Power was from the mortar power station, the central power plant or from commercial sources. Data transmission was by telephone. It was turned over to Artillery May 22, 1907. Guns and carriages were removed sometime after March 1946.

BATTERY WORTH

Named for Brigadier General William Scott Worth. He was brevetted captain August 1, 1864 for gallant and meritorious service in the assault of enemy lines before Petersburg, and brevetted April 9, 1865, during the Appomattox campaign. He took part in the attack on San Juan Hill July 1, 1898, in which he was wounded. While recovering he was appointed brigadier general of volunteers, July 12, 1898. He died October 16, 1904.

Two 10-inch rifles mounted on disappearing carriages: The emplacements were built between September 1897 and the end 1898 at a cost of $51,047.23. Data transmission was by telephone. Power supply was from station #3 Battery Moore or from commercial sources. It was turned over to the Artillery on June 16, 1902. Guns and carriages were declared "no longer required" on February 23, 1933. The guns were declared obsolete armament during the "Salvage of Obsolete Armament" movement and were cut up for scrap and removed October 24, 1942.

FIXED A-A 1920

The 1st Aerial Battery was located at the North end of the reservation by the upper gate. It was turned over to the Artillery on September 23, 1920 even though the guns weren't installed until 1922. Power source was an Edison type A-4 6-volt storage battery. The Battery was disarmed of guns and carriages in July 1936.

The 2nd Aerial Battery was located between Crockett Lake and the main road into the fort. It was turned over September 23, 1920 even though the guns weren't installed until 1922. Power source was an Edison type A-4 6-volt storage battery. The Battery was disarmed of guns and carriages in 1937 and moved to form a new fixed emplacement atop the former Kingsbury and Moore batteries.

Four 3-inch antiaircraft guns making up two batteries were built between June 1, 1920 and November 1922 when base rings for gun tubes were set. The cost for both batteries was $972.35.

MOBILE-FIXED A-A 1937

Three 3-inch mobile antiaircraft guns were installed in 1937. These were mobile or moveable gun batteries located in the fields below the mortars. They were turned over to the Artillery on October 11, 1937, and cost $564.19. Power supply was a portable electric generator that was daily moved to the battery location. The guns were originally mobile but were installed for permanent use after World War II began. These three guns were moved between September 1942 and January 1943 and relocated to the former 10-inch gun emplacements Kingsbury and Moore.

FIXED-A-A 1943

This battery of 3-3-inch antiaircraft guns were moved from their former location in the lower fields below the mortars to the empty gun pits of Kingsbury #1 & 2 and Moore #3. Part of the rooms under the gun emplacements were converted for use as quarters, rest rooms, and ammunition storage. The move and construction of the AA Director and other support structures cost $14,000. The battery was turned over to the artillery on June 14, 1943. Power supply was by AA director generating units M-IV and commercial power. There was no direct source at the Battery site. Data transmission was by AA Director M-IV. The guns were removed in 1944.

APPENDIX B

FORT CASEY'S MAIN ARMAMENT

THE 10-INCH DISAPPEARING RIFLE

THE 12-INCH MORTAR

SECONDARY ARMAMENT

THE 6-INCH DISAPPEARING RIFLE

5-INCH SEACOST GUN ON BALANCED PILLAR MOUNT

3-INCH PEDESTAL MOUNTED RAPID FIRE RIFLE

FIRING SEQUENCES: DISAPPEARING RIFLE

ABOVE: A 12-inch disappearing rifle at a coast artillery fortification on the East Coast. The man with his back to us with the large bucket is the barrel swabber. He used the large mop like swab to wash out the barrel of any remaining burning powder embers before the next shell is loaded.

BELOW: The loading crew is ramming the next projectile from the shot cart into the barrel. While this is going on the men on top of the gun are checking the firing area for potential obstructions such as a friendly ship accidentally sailing into the training area.

ABOVE: The two men on the left have the next shell cart ready for loading. The 12" projectile is on the top of the cart and the two powder bags are on the bottom.

BELOW: While the shell is being loaded into the breech other men on the left are setting the elevation and direction of the rifle so it is ready once the counterweight is tripped and the gun rises up to fire.

ABOVE, BELOW: The powder and shell have been loaded into the gun, the breech is about to be closed and men are scrambling to get out of the way as the weapon is prepared for firing. The counterweight has been tripped, it drops into the well under the carriage, and the huge barrel is raised to the firing position over the walls of the emplacement. The men on top of the gun are bracing themselves for firing.

ABOVE, BELOW: The gun fires and begins its descent back to the loading position from the recoil of the discharge. The men are standing on their tiptoes with their mouths open to relieve the tremendous pressure created by the blast. Standing on tiptoes prevented you from being knocked over by the concussion.

FIRING SEQUENCES: 12-INCH MORTAR

LEFT: A 12-inch mortar the moment after it has been fired. The tip of the shell is just emerging from the barrel. Notice how the men in the pit are standing, some holding their ears but all braced and at angles to the gun. Because of the design of the mortar pits the heat, the noise, and the concussion were all magnified and could easily knock a man over if they weren't ready. It was described by one veteran as, "Feeling like someone hit you with a soaking wet towel." This mortar pit is at an East Coast fort.

RIGHT: The first bit of smoke begins to emerge from the barrel surrounding the shell. The 700 pound projectile is being pushed out of the mortar barrel by the explosion of the silk bag of nitrocellulose. A shot cart is at the bottom of the picture ready for the reloading and next firing.

LEFT: The mushroom cloud begins to form as the escaping gas of the powder explosion overtakes the shell. Shell carts are standing at the ready for the next firing.

RIGHT: The mushroom cloud at its fullest with the shell still not visible yet.

LEFT: The mushroom gives way to the flash of the expanding gas of the blast. The mortar is in full recoil and will drop down to the loading position. The guns were designed to only fire in the raised or up position to prevent any possible misfiring into the pits.

The expanding flash grows bigger. Notice how the shirts of the men are all pressed against their bodies. That is the concussion wave hitting them.

RIGHT: The flash cloud of smoke grown bigger and light up the entire pit.

The shell emerges from the powder flash and begins climbing over the top of the emplacement. The mortar pits were designed to be completely protected from direct line fire as they were built behind the emplacement walls and high bank hillsides.

CHAPTER FOOTNOTES

CHAPTER ONE

[1] Emanuel Raymond Lewis, *Seacoast Fortifications of the United States: An Introductory History* (City of Washington: Smithsonian Institute Press, 1970), p. 100.

[2] Russell F. Weigley, *Towards and American Army* (New York: Columbia University Press, 1962), chapters 5 and 9.

[3] John M. Blum, et al. *The National Experience* (New York: Harcourt, Brace and World, Inc., 1968), pp. 110-111.

[4] Joseph M. Bailey, "The Defenses of Puget Sound," (typewritten paper, Washington State Library, Olympia, 1966), p. 2.

[5] Emanuel Raymond Lewis, *Seacoast Fortifications of the United States: An Introductory History* (City of Washington: Smithsonian Institute Press, 1970), pp. 4-5.

[6] Russell F. Weigley, *History of the United States Army* (New York: Macmillan Company, 1967), p. 284.

[7] James D. Richardson, ed., *A Complication of the Messages and Papers of the Presidents* (10 vols. and supplements; Washington: Government Printing office, 1907), vol. 9, pp. 728-729.

[8] Lewis, *Seacoast Fortifications*, p.6.

[9] V. J. Gregory, *Keepers at the Gate* (Port Townsend: Port Townsend Pub. Co., Inc., 1976), p. 39.

[10] 37th Congress: 2nd Session, House Report No. 86 (Ser. 1145), 420-421; 50th Congress, 1st Session, Senate Ex. Doc. No. 165 (Ser. 2513), 61-63.

[11] John A. Hussey: "A Short History of Fort Casey, Washington" (typewritten manuscript, National Parks Service, 1956), p. 13-14.

[12] 50th Congress: 1st Session, Senate Ex. Doc. No. 165 (Ser. 2513), p. 73.

[13] Ibid, p.74.

[14] Dorothy O. Johansen, *Empire of the Columbia* (New York: Harper & Row, 1957), p. 253.

[15] Ray Theodore Cowell, "History of Fort Townsend," in *Washington Historical Quarterly*, XVI (October 1925), pp. 284-285.

[16] Hussey, "Short History of Fort Casey," p. 15.

[17] Murray, Keith A., *The Pig War* (Tacoma: Washington State Historical Society, 1968), pp. 15-22.

[18] 50th Congress: 1st Session, Senate Ex. Doc. No. 165 (Ser. 2513), pp. 64-65.

[19] General Totten, at age 72, had been the Army's Chief Engineer since 1838 and was one of the nations' most respected military minds. He had earned an international reputation in the development of nineteenth century seacoast fortifications and the official observations he made would dominate military thinking concerning coastal defense and the Puget Sound for years thereafter.

[20] 50th Congress: Senate Ex. Doc. No. 165, p.53.

[21] Ibid.

[22] Ibid, pp. 54-55.

[23] Ibid, p. 60.

[24] Ibid, p. 40.

[25] Lewis, *Seacoast Fortifications*, p. 66.

[26] Ibid, p. 67.

[27] Ibid,

[28] Ian Hogg, *The History of Fortification* (New York: St. Martin's Press, Inc., 1981), p. 144.

[29] The pointed projectiles had several advantages over the spherical cannon-balls fired by smoothbore guns. These advantages were mainly due to the fact that an elongated projectile comprises a far greater mass than a sphere of the same diameter, but does not encounter a corresponding increase in air resistance during its flight. It was also now possible to obtain a greater degree of accuracy, since the projectile adhered more closely to its theoretical trajectory. In other words, rifled guns could deliver against a given target much larger effective impact energies than smoothbores, at substantially greater ranges, and in general, with greater accuracy. Rifled artillery could do easily what smoothbores could achieve only after long, tedious bombardments. See also Lewis, *Seacoast Fortifications*, pp. 66-68 for further explanations.

[30] Ibid, p. 42.

[31] Hogg, *History of Fortification*, p. 174.

[32] Ibid,

[33] Ibid, p. 175.

[34] Ian Hogg, *Coast Defenses of England and Wales: 1856-1956* (London: David & Charles, 1974), p, 18.

[35] Unsuccessful attempts by combined French-British fleets in 1855 against the harbor defenses of Kronstadt pointed out the obvious strength of a well-constructed and well-armed fort. Against what seemed to be overwhelming odds, the fortifications not only resisted but took a heavy toll on the attacking fleet. Another action that took place in October, 1855, however provided much different results. In this instance the combined fleets used armored floating batteries to bombard the coastal fortifications at Kinburn. The vessels were covered with four inches of iron plating over

seventeen inches of wood. With this protection the French ships were able to anchor only 800 yards from their targets began systematically shelling the fort. After some four hours of shelling, the interior of the fort had been demolished with comparatively little return damage done to the armored ships. The Russian commander surrendered; the fleet moved across and took up its position off Fort Ochakov. The commander of that work capitulated forthwith, without waiting to be bombarded. The successful use by combined French-British fleets of armored gun platforms at Kinburn convinced the French that armored ships were not only practical but the future of naval architecture. This lead to the launching of the French iron-clad warship *La Gloire* in 1858.
Ian Hogg, *Fortress*, (New York: St. Martin's Press, Inc., 1975), p. 82.

[36] Hogg, *History of Fortifications*, p. 146.

[37] The technical lessons gathered from the Civil War sent English engineers toward masses of iron coverings. The sea forts in particular were surrounded with iron cladding up to seven inches thick. They also began drafting plans for the construction of entirely new, and extremely expensive, types of permanent harbor defenses armored with layers of iron as well as iron turrets.

[38] Lewis, *Seacoast Fortifications*, p. 68.

[39] Ibid,

[40] For further details on the competitions and trials see Hogg, *Fortress*, pp. 92-94.

[41] As the iron age of fortifications began, masonry walls were the standard. To give added protection for both men and equipment iron shields were installed over the gun ports. This then led to installing armor plating over the stone walls themselves and ultimately to having parts of the forts being totally constructed out of iron. The continuous iron casemates gave way to armored turrets and finally to the more streamlined cupolas of solid metal. Ingenious engineers developed ways to retract and even to oscillate the cupolas to increase their protection and firing ability. Eventually the designers began to recess both the gun cupolas and the majority of the forts themselves behind vast earthen walls. By 1880 massive works in France, Belgium, and Germany were following this pattern of subterranean fortifications with armored cupolas.

[42] Lewis, *Seacoast Fortifications*, p. 69.

[43] Ibid, pp. 69-70.

[44] Ibid, p.70.

[45] Ibid, p. 75.

[46] Steel is an alloy of mixed metals that proved much stronger than cast iron in the making of gun barrels. Cast iron was a suitable metal for smoothbore ordnance, but did not have the needed strength for rifled weapons. Iron simply could not withstand the increased pressure generated within the bore when the gun was fired. As the size of smoothbore weapons increased, cast iron molded guns reached a practical limit beyond which additional thickness added to the walls of the gun would add little to the ability of the piece to withstand pressure. The giant 15-inch Rodman guns developed during the Civil War were considered the culmination of smoothbore ordnance. With the coming of the iron-clad age and the need for weapons with greater power and penetration a metal stronger than iron was sought. The introduction of rifling within the

barrel and the new, more powerful types of powder being developed also pointed to the need for something stronger than iron in heavy ordnance. The problem was to increase power but not the weight and bore of the gun. The evolution of steel eventually answered this problem. It was not until after the Civil War, however, that the domestic metal industry reached a state of maturity that would enable ordnance manufacturers to produce these new weapons. The knowledge had been available for a number of years but it was not technologically possible until many years after the Civil War. See Lewis Chapter 3 on Modern Era or Rogers, *History of Artillery*, chapters 8 & 9 for more on technological improvements.

[47] Lewis, *Seacoast Fortifications*, p. 75.

[48] Varying degrees of success had been achieved by the Armstrong Ordnance Company in England and by Krupp in Germany but only in light cannon. The great difficulty was in designing a breech mechanism that could withstand the repeated extremes of temperature and gas pressures and yet still be worked with some speed by the gun crew. Added to this was the development of new, longer guns. In seacoast forts and particularly on ships there just was not room enough to roll the guns back far enough to load powder and shot with their longer barrels. Because of this demand for more space with the new weapons, the perfection of breech-loading in heavy ordnance was essential.

[49] Lewis, *Seacoast Fortifications*, p. 75.

[50] Ibid, p. 76.

[51] The traditionally-used gunpowder burned very quickly when ignited which made it an ideal propellant for the relatively short barreled smoothbore guns. Firing trials with the new, long guns, however, showed that gunpowder did not deliver a consistent enough force. A constant explosive pressure was needed against the projectile as it moved along the entire length of the gun barrel. This was achieved through the use of new propellants such as picric acid and trinitrotoluene (TNT) and by reshaping the powder grains into the form of hexagonal prisms instead of the normal granular shape. By using powder in this form it was now possible to control the rate at which the propellant within the gun tube burned, instead of exploding all at once, these new powders could be regulated to explode more slowly and thus provide a continual push against the shell as it moved down the barrel.

[52] Lewis, *Seacoast Fortifications*, p. 76.

[53] Hogg, *Fortress*, p. 110.

[54] Gregory, *Keepers at the Gate*, p. 81.

[55] Edward Mead Earle, ed., *Makers of Modern Strategy* (Princeton: Princeton University Press, 1952), p. 434.

[56] The writings of Alfred Thayer Mahan had a great influence not only on military men but on aspiring political leaders as well. Rising statesmen such as Henry Cabot Lodge and Theodore Roosevelt were strong supporters of the Mahan theories of Navalism. Through his writings and the work of men like Roosevelt and Lodge, who believed in him and agitated for a big navy, Mahan helped to shape a new naval policy for America. His command-of-the-seas concepts began to gain widespread circulation and with the Naval Act of 1890, which authorized the building

of three new battleships to go along with the two begun in 1886, the government announced to the world its intention of building a navy that would be a legitimate sea power. In the years that followed there was a steady increase in the reconstruction of the fleet and its movement away from protecting the coasts. Roosevelt's election to the presidency in 1901 allowed him to continue pushing for a larger, more powerful Navy and to eliminate the passive coast-defense doctrine from naval policy once and for all.

[57] 50th Congress, Senate Ex. Doc. No. 165, pp. 17-22.

[58] Ibid, p. 16.

[59] Barry M. Gough, *The Royal Navy and the Northwest Coast of North America*, 1810-1914 (Vancouver, University of British Columbia Press, 1971), p. 167.

[60] 49th Congress: 1st Session, House Exec. Doc. No. 49 (Ser. 2395, 2396), pp. 8, 24, 25.

[61] Hogg, *History of Fortifications*, p. 177.

[62] 50th Congress, Senate Ex. Doc. No. 165, pp. 1-3.

[63] Ibid, p. 4.

[64] Ibid, pp. 1-3.

[65] "Establishing the Navy Yard, Puget Sound" *Washington Historical Quarterly*, Vol. II, (October, 1907), pp. 356-357.

CHAPTER TWO

[1] Donation claims referred to the government policy of either giving or selling, on liberal terms, land in underdeveloped areas to encourage settlement.

[2] John A. Hussey, "A Short History of Fort Casey, Washington" (typewritten manuscript, National Parks Service, 1956), p. 28. It is interesting to note that the State of Washington, in granting the United States the use of the tidelands on the shores of Admiralty Inlet and Admiralty Bay, inserted the proviso that such use should revert to the state whenever the government should discontinue holding the abutting uplands for certain specific public purposes. *See footnote 3. This proviso concerning tidelands would come to light again in 1954 when the larger part of the reservation would be declared surplus property.

[3] Hussey, "A Short History of Fort Casey", p. 32.

[4] U.S. War Dept., *Military Reservations*, Wash., 2, 11-12.

[5] 55th Cong., 2nd Sess., "House Document" No. 2. Report of Chief of Engineers, Part I (Serial 3631), 21.

[6] George Albert Kellogg, A History of Whidbey's Island (Island County Historical Society, Island County, Washington, 1934), p. 96.

[7] Weekly report of Hired Labor employed at Admiralty Head, week of Jan 30, 1898, Philip G. Eastwick, assistant engineer, to District Office, Corps of Engineers. Class of labor and rate of pay per hour.

CLASS OF LABOR	RATE OF PAY	HOW EMPLOYED
carpenters	25¢	building trestle
carpenters	20¢	building trestle
foreman	25¢	building trestle
laborers	15¢	building trestle
carpenters	25¢	trolley line
foreman	25¢	trolley line
laborers	15¢	trolley line
pipeman	35¢	laying sewer pipe
laborers	15¢	laying pipe
carpenters	25¢	wharf const.
carpenters	20¢	wharf const.
foreman	25¢	wharf
laborers	15¢	wharf
teams	20¢	miscellaneous
teamsters	15¢	miscellaneous
laborers	15¢	miscellaneous
blacksmith	20¢	miscellaneous
carpenters	25¢	miscellaneous
teams	20¢	grading
teamsters	16¢	grading
laborers	15¢	grading

It makes one wonder if the carpenters and the foremen, who were the ones benefiting most from the pay increase, were the strike leaders or if the Corps of Engineers was doing its best to save money at the men's expense.

[8] Monthly report, Philip G. Eastwick to Lieut. M. L. Walker, Corps of Engineers, March 3, 1898.

[9] Watson C. Squire, Military Posts on Puget Sound, Speech in the Senate of the United States, February 28, 1895 (Washington, 1895), 4-5.

[10] James G. McCurdy, By Juan de Fuca's Strait (Portland, Oregon, 1937), 306-307.

[11] Hussy, "Short History of Fort Casey", p. 39.

[12] United States, War Dept., Military Reservations, Wash. (Washington, 1942), 11-12. As a First Lieutenant, he had made surveys of the Admiralty Head area that were later adopted. A graduate of the United States Military Academy, Casey in his long career with the Corps of Engineers was supervisor of many well-known projects. He is best remembered for his work in the nation's capital.

Under his direction such notable projects as the Washington Monument, the Patomac Aqueduct, and the Library of Congress were built. Upon his death in March of 1896 many officers and private citizens were saddened.

[13] Letter from Assistant Engineer, Sampson P. Mason to Lieut. M. L. Walker, Corps of Engineers, Seattle, Wash., February 7, 1900, informing them of the transfer of the post to the Army.

[14] Corps of Engineers, Fiscal Report for year 1900. Lieutenant M. L. Walker, Corps of Engineers Seattle, to Captain Harry Taylor, operations director, June 30, 1900. Corps of Engineers files, Record Group 77, Box 293. National Archives, Seattle-Branch.

[15] Corps of Engineers files, miscellaneous construction documents, Record Group 77. National Archives, Seattle-Branch.

[16] Ibid.

[17] Corps of Engineers files, monthly letter from Sampson D. Mason, Inspector, to Lieut. M. L. Walker, Corps of Engineers, Seattle. Record Group 77, miscellaneous documents. National Archives, Seattle-Branch.

[18] Plans and specifications for Admiralty Head, Wash., Light Station, Prepared by Engineers office, 13th L. H. District, Portland, Oregon, July 5, 1901...MSS (13 sheets in custody of Seattle Office, GSA). The old lighthouse had been sitting silently in the field to the north of the main emplacements where it had been moved when construction had first begun in 1897. It would stay there for many years to come before it was eventually torn down by a retiring post soldier and rebuilt elsewhere on Whidbey Island. The new lighthouse was to be quite an elaborate structure. It was to have a circular brick tower, about 25 feet high, and would be connected to a sturdy, two-story brick keeper's house. A number of smaller structures were also built along with this new aid to navigation at Admiralty Head.

[19] Map of Fort Casey, Wash., showing boundaries of Present Reservation and Additional land required, to accompany Report of Board of officers, convened by Par. 18, S.O. No. 55, Headquarters of the Army, March 7, 1900 (In Seattle Office, GSA).

[20] Map Exhibit "A" Fort Casey, Wash., to accompany Report of Board of officers convened by paragraph 1 5.0. 35, Headquarters, Dept, of the Columbia, February 20th, 1902 (in Seattle Office, GSA).

[21] *P.I.* (Seattle), March 2; August 23, 1903; Corps of Engineers, Fort Casey Construction Data Index, MSS (bound group of 9 sheets, in Seattle Office, GSA).

[22] Corps of Engineers, Fort Casey, Construction Data Index, MSS; Whiting, *Forts of Washington*, p. 29.

[23] General Order No. 194, War Dept., Washington, December 27, 1904, Paragraph 198, Army Regulations.

[24] Corps of Engineers, Monthly Report to Corps of Engineers Headquarters, Seattle, Wash., December 11, 1909. Official documents dated January 1, 1910, list the following armament of the batteries at Fort Casey with their total cost of construction to that point. All batteries were completed and in service.

NAME OF BATTERY	ARMAMENT	COST
John Valleau	4x6-inch rifles	$92,125.00
Thomas Parker	2x6-inch rifles	$50,380.00
John Trevor	2x3-inch rapid fire	$15,800.00
Issac Van Horne	2x3-inch rapid fire	$14,695.00
Reuben Turman	2x5-inch rapid fire	$18,850.00
Truman Seymour	8x12-inch mortars	$46,603.00
Alexander Schenck	8x12-inch mortars	$46,603.00
William Worth	2x10-inch rifles	$51,057.00
James Moore	3x10-inch rifles	$98,078.00
Henry Kingsbury	2x10-inch rifles	$92,261.00

Total cost for the 35 guns comprising the ten batteries in service at Fort Casey was $526,452.00.

CHAPTER THREE

[1] Ian Hogg, *The History of Fortification* (New York: St. Martin's Press, Inc., 1981), p. 177.

[2] Ibid.

[3] Ian Hogg, *Coast Defences of England and Wales: 1856-1956* (North Pomfret, Vermont, David & Charles, Inc., 1974), pp, 76-77.

[4] Emanuel Raymond Lewis, *Seacoast Fortifications of the United States: An Introductory History* (City of Washington: Smithsonian Institute Press, 1970), p. 80.

[5] Ibid.

[6] Ibid., p. 83.

[7] Ibid., p. 95.

[8] Ibid.

[9] In 1907 the number of seacoast units was increased to 170 and the two artillery components gained formal recognition as distinct branches of the Army. The two would remain separate until 1950 when the two units would be reunited into a single Artillery Branch. During this period the Coast Artillery became synonymous as the corps of artillery specialists.

[10] Corps of Engineers: miscellaneous files dealing with improvements and completed construction, January 6, 1904; Record Group 77, boxes 241 to 248, National Archives, Seattle-Branch.

[11] Lewis, *Seacoast Fortifications*, p. 89.

[12] Ibid., p. 93.

[13] Corps of Engineers files: miscellaneous documents on improvements and construction of Central Power Plant; Record Group 77, boxes 298 to 307, National Archives, Seattle-Branch.

[14] John M. Blum, et al. *The National Experience* (New York: Harcourt, Brace and World, Inc., 1968), p. 520.

[15] Russell F. Weigley, *History of the United States Army* (New York: Macmillian Company, 1967), p. 284.

[16] Blum, *National Experience*, p. 521.

[17] Lewis, *Seacoast Fortifications*, p. 98.

[18] Blum, *National Experience*, p. 521. Mahan was the prophet of world power for the United States, and was heard and honored by many. Counted among his disciples were Theodore Roosevelt and Henry Cabot Lodge. They were the agitators for a big Navy and a more dominate role for America in world politics.

[19] V, J. Gregory, *Keepers at the Gate* (Port Townsend: Port Townsend Pub. Co., Inc., 1976), p. 85.

[20] Harold L. Peterson, *Forts in America* (New York: Charles Scriber's Son's, 1964), p. 60.

[21] Joseph M. Bailey, "The Defenses of Puget Sound," (Typewritten paper, Washington State Library, Olympia, 1966), p. 2.

[22] Corps of Engineers: Miscellaneous documents concerning troop strength in connection with availability of housing, Record Group 77, boxes 298 to 307; National Archives, Seattle-Branch.

[23] Special Report, "Report on Preparedness Pacific Coast Artillery District", June 30, 1913, Corps of Engineers; Seattle, Washington.

[24] Jimmie Jean Cook, *A particular friend, Penn's Cove* (Coupeville, Washington: Island County Historical Society, 1973), p. 109.

[25] Mickey Clark, private interview held in Coupeville, Washington, April 2, 1985.

[26] Corps of Engineer files; miscellaneous documents concerning daily activities at the fort, reports of practice firings of various weapons, and accuracy reports from target practice competitions: Record Group 77, boxes 314 to 325 and 298 to 307; National Archives, Seattle-Branch. A great deal of information concerning daily activities at the post also came from personal interviews with Frank Thesenvitz, a soldier stationed at Fort Casey, and from Mickey Clark, who was born at the fort and has spent his entire life in the Coupeville area.

[27] Gregory, *Keepers at the Gate*, chapter 15.

[28] Corps of Engineer files: miscellaneous documents concerning target practices; Record Group 77, boxes 314 to 325 and 298 to 307; National Archives, Seattle-Branch. In interviewing soldiers who were stationed at Fort Casey the reputation of their ability to accurately hit targets during target practice was repeated over and over again. How true some of the stories are I have no way to verify but most seem to be true. One reputation in particular that was repeated in at least three different interviews was the ability of the big 10-inch gun crews to knock seagulls off logs at a range of 1,000 yards. Many of the men also claimed that the crews could hit just about any target in three shots; one over, one under, and one right on. In any event, the soldiers who were stationed at Casey practiced daily with the guns for months on end.

[29] Gregory, *Keepers at the Gate*, pp. 138-139.

[30] Corps of Engineer files: Miscellaneous documents, letter from Lieutenant Colonel E. Eveleth Winslow to Chief of Engineers, Washington, December 28, 1915; Record Group 77, boxes 298 to 307; National Archives, Seattle-Branch.

[31] Major Charles Edward Kirkpatrick, *Archie in the A.E.F.: The Creation of the Antiaircraft Service of the United States Army, 1917-1918*, (US Army Air Defense Artillery School, 1984), pp. 2, 4, 6.

[32] "Christmas Menu 1916," from personal collection of Mickey Clark, Coupeville, Washington, p. 10.

CHAPTER FOUR

[1] Annual Report of the Secretary of War, 1908, Serial 5420, p. 28.

[2] David M. Hansen, "The Regulars and the Militia in the Coast Defenses of Puget Sound," *Military Influences of Washington History*, proceedings of a conference, March 29-31, 1984, p. 120.

[3] Russel F. Weigley, *History of the United States Army* (New York: Macmillian Company, 1967), p. 10.

[4] Jess VanDemark, private interview held in Ferndale, Washington, July, 1988.

[5] Frank Thesenvitz, private interview held in Seattle, November 25, 1970.

[6] Henry Juvet, private interview held in Ferndale, Washington, July, 1988.

[7] Ibid., interview.

[8] Ibid.

[9] Interview, Thesenvitz.

[10] Ibid.

[11] Interview, Juvet.

[12] Interview, Thesenvitz.

[13] Ibid.

[14] Interview, Juvet.

[15] Ibid.

[16] Interview, Thesenvitz.

[17] Gregory, *Keepers at the Gate*, pp. 96-97.

[18] Ibid, pp 161-166.

[19] Interview, Thesenvitz.

CHAPTER FIVE

[1] John M. Blum, et al. *The National Experience* (New York: Harcourt, Brace and World, Inc., 1968), pp. 593-594.

[2] Emanuel Raymond Lewis, *Seacoast fortifications of the United States: An Introductory History* (City of Washington: Smithsonian Institute Press, 1970), p. 100.

[3] Corps of Engineers files: miscellaneous documents dealing with future used for guns no longer needed or obsolete, May 15, 1917; Record Group 77, boxes 298 to 307 and 314 to 325.

[4] Ibid., Removal of guns, September and October 1917. For some reason, gun #2 of Battery Kingsbury, (#7 if all 7 guns are considered as the main emplacement), was removed from its carriage in early 1909. The 10-inch gun tube was taken down from the parapet and then placed on skids. This was pulled by mules to a location between the first of Battery Valleau's gun emplacements and the main road overpass. The gun was sealed to prevent rusting within the barrel and left to sit. It was later moved when one of the searchlight power houses was built where it had been sitting but from 1909 until 1918 it remained sitting idly on the ground. Its gun carriage in Battery Kingsbury was weatherized and attended to but sat empty throughout World War I.

[5] Ibid., May 3, 1919 on gun removal.

[6] Ibid., miscellaneous files dealing with construction of AA batteries during 1920.

[7] At Fort Casey the troop assignments were made by Battery:

COMPANY	BATTERY	STRENGTH
9th Reg. Army	Seymour	170 men
10th Reg. Army	Worth	170 men
11th Reg. Army	Schenck	170 men
12th Reg. Army	Searchlights & communications	132 men
18th Nat. Guard	Kingsbury	66 men
25th Nat. Guard	Moore	66 men
28th Nat. Guard	Van Horne	66 men
31st A.E.F.	Moore	132 men
35th A.E.F.	Worth	66 men
36th A.E.F.	Turman	66 men
37th A.E.F.	Kingsbury	66 men
40th A.E.F.	Trevor	66 men

[8] V. J. Gregory, *Keepers at the Gate* (Port Townsend: Port Townsend Pub. Co., Inc., 1976), p. 145.

[9] Constance McLaughlin Green, Harry Thomson, and Peter C. Root, *The Ordnance Department: Planning Munitions for War* (Washington D. C.: U. S. Government Printing office, 1955), p. 30.

[10] Gregory, *Keepers*, p. 185.

[11] Gregory, *Keepers*, pp. 185-186.

[12] Corps of Engineers files: miscellaneous documents dealing with A.A. construction between 1920 and March 2, 1923; Record Group 141; boxes 117 to 127, National Archives, Suitland-Branch.

[13] Major H. H. Arnold, "Post War Development of Aerial Observation of Artillery Fire," *Journal of the United States Artillery*, Vol. 55, No. 6 (December, 1921), p. 509.

[14] Gregory, *Keepers*, p. 204.

[15] Ibid.

[16] Ibid.

[17] Ibid.

[18] Corps of Engineers files: miscellaneous documents; Record group 77, boxes 117 to 127; National Archives, Suitland-Branch. It was very difficult to pin down an exact date of demolition for the hangar. The Corps records are sketchy since the structure was under the Signal Corps. The removal date is arrived at by comparing Fort structure inventories done in 1938 and 1940. Also through recollections of local residents who lost their sheltered tennis court when it was removed.

[19] Erna Risch, *Quartermaster Support of the Army: A History of the Corps 1775-1939* (Washington D. C.: U. S. Government Printing Office, 1962), p. 711.

[20] Corps of Engineers files: miscellaneous documents dealing with discipline, maintenance cutbacks, and the neglect of the fort that was becoming visible. From mid-1924 through 1927 then fort officially went on caretaker status; Record Group 77, boxes 300 to 305 and 314 to 325; National Archives, Seattle-Branch.

[21] Gregory, *Keepers*, p. 188.

[22] Corps of Engineers files: miscellaneous documents covering monthly activities; Record Group 77, boxes 298 to 307; National Archives, Seattle-Branch.

[23] Francis Russell, *The Shadow of Blooming Grove* (New McGraw Hill, 1968), p. 588.

[24] U.S. Navy JAG records: Record Group 125. Board of Inquiry results of the *Zeilen-Henderson* collision issued 1924; National Archives, Suitland-Branch.

[25] Mickey Clark, private interview heldin Coupeville, Washington, April 29, 1985.

[26] Gregory, *Keepers*, p. 193.

[27] Ibid., p. 196.

[28] Ibid.

[29] Special Letter; "Status of Coast Defenses", July 13, 1927, Corps of Engineers files; Seattle, Washington.

[30] Billie Smith, private interview held in Coupeville, Washington, April 21, 1985.

[31] Russell F. Wrigley, *History of the United States Army* (Bloomington: Indiana University Press, 1967), p. 402.

[32] Ibid., p. 403.

[33] Corps of Engineers files: miscellaneous documents concerning improvements in Switchboard house and the new radio equipment; Dated August 11, 1933; Record Group 77, boxes 117 to 127; National Archives, Suitland-Branch.

[34] Frank Thesenvitz, private interview held inSeattle, Washington, November 25, 1970.

CHAPTER SIX

[1] Russell F. Weigley, *History of the United States Army* (Bloomington: Indiana University Press, 1967), p. 403.

[2] Ibid., p. 416.

[3] Special Letter: "Status of Coast Defenses," July 13, 1927, Corps of Engineers files, Seattle, Washington.

[4] Corps of Engineers files: miscellaneous documents dealing with monthly inspections of Fort Casey. One of particular notes that summarized many of the problems of neglect was on May 16, 1928, from H. H. Pritchett, Assistant Corps Area Inspector to the War Dept. Record Group 77, boxes 117 to 127; National Archives, Suitland-Branch.

[5] Ibid., specifically from July 13, 1927 to July 22, 1939.

[6] Article, *Seattle Times*, March 6, 1938.

[7] Lenore Fine and Jesse A. Remmington, *The United States Army in World War II, Corps of Engineers: Construction in the United States* (Washington, D.C.: Office of the Chief of Military History, 1972), p. 74.

[8] Weigley, *History of the Army*, p. 419.

[9] Byron Fairchild and Stetson Conn, *The United States Army in World War II, The Western Hemisphere: The Framework of Hemisphere Defense:* (Washington D.C.: Office of the Chief of Military History, 1960), p 15.

[10] Weigley, *History of the Army*, p. 420.

[11] Ibid., p. 423.

[12] Ibid., p. 424.

[13] John M. Blum, *et at. The National Experience* (New York: Harcourt, Brace and World, Inc., 1968), p. 726.

[14] Corps of Engineers files: miscellaneous documents concerning the Modernization Program, September 1, 1940 through September 6, 1943; Record Group 77, boxes 120 to 127; National Archives, Suitland-Branch.

[15] Don Lee, private interview held in Coupeville, Washington, May 4, 1985.

[16] The two searchlights located at the north end of the reservation, near the upper gate, and the two below the main emplacements would be maintained. The fifth light, which had been mounted on a 25-foot tower on the beach along Crockett's Lake, had fallen victim to the lack of care and had already been removed. Not long after this report was made searchlight number 11 became unsafe for use due to the undermining of the bluff on which it was located. The light was removed and the Fort operated with just 3 fixed lights.

[17] The gas proofing was to be done to latrines, rest rooms (rooms at the gun emplacements where the men took breaks from duty and had meals), plotting rooms, first aide stations, and the fire control center.

[18] Special Report; "Review of Harbor Defenses in Puget Sound in connection with the Modernization Program," January, 1941. Corps of Engineers files: miscellaneous documents; Record Group 77, box 126; National Archives, Suitland-Branch.

[19] Fairchild and Conn, *Hemisphere Defense*, p. 43.

[20] Special Report, "Review of Modernization Program, Puget Sound, 1941-1945," Corps of Engineer files, Washington D.C.

[21] Roy Engom, private interview held in Oak Harbor, Washington, November 8, 1970.

[22] Richard Izban, private interview held in Anacortes, Washington, April 5, 1985.

[23] Emerson Jelele, private interview held in Oak Harbor, Washington, July 9, 1988.

[24] Weigley, *History of the Army*, p. 432

[25] Lee, interview.

[26] Izban, interview.

[27] Engom, interview.

[28] Jedele, interview.

[29] Ibid.

[30] Lee, interview.

[32] Grahame F. Strader, *The Phantom War in the Northwest*, (Washington: GPD, 1969), p. 7.

[32] Me1 Bates, private interview held in Anacortes, Washington, April 13, 1985. Also Don Lee interview and the Roy Engom interview.

[33] Izban, interview.

[34] Engom, interview.

[35] Me1 Bates, interview.

[36] Billie Smith, private interview held in Coupeville, Washington, April 21, 1985.

[37] Bates, interview.

[38] Article; *Seattle Times*, fall 1970. Also Corps of Engineers files: miscellaneous documents dated June 21, 1942, concerning the attack; Record Group 77, boxes 124-125; National Archives, Suitland-Branch. Gregory, *Keepers at the Gate*, has a further account of the shelling, pp. 221-222.

[39] Izban, interview.

[40] Corps of Engineers files: miscellaneous documents on Modernization Program from January 1942 to June 16, 1943 when the Program was termed completed; Record Group 77, boxes 122 to 127; National Archives, Suitland-Branch.

[41] Ibid., also Don Lee interview.

[42] Engom, interview.

[43] Jedele, interview.

[44] Joseph M. Bailey: "TheDefenses of PugetSound," (typewritten paper, Washington State Library, Olympia, 1966), p. 2.

[45] Engom, interview.

[46] Corps of Engineers files: miscellaneous documents dealing with Modernization program.

[47] Engom, interview.

[48] Lee, interview.

[49] Donald Sutton, private interview held in Anacortes, Washington, April 3, 1985.

[50] Bates, interview.

[51] Izban, interview.

[52] Blum, *The National Experience*, p. 750.

[53] Corps of Engineers files: miscellaneous documents concerning movement of Battery G 14th Coast Artillery from Worden to Casey for specialized training, June 25, 1943 to September 18, 1944; Record Group 77, Boxes 125 to 127; National Archives, Suitland-Branch, Also Donald Sutton interview.

[54] Lee, interview.

[55] Sutton, interview.

[56] Emanuel Raymond Lewis, *Seacoast Fortifications of the United States: An Introductory History* (City of Washington: Smithsonian Institute Press, 1970), p. 124.

[57] Ibid.

CHAPTER SEVEN

[1] Emanuel Raymond Lewis, *Seacoast Fortifications of the United States: An introductory History* (City of Washington: Smithsonian Institute Press, 1970), p. 124.

[2] Daryl Franzen, private interview held in Coupeville, Washington, August 2, 1988.

[3] Article, *Seattle Times*, April 17, 1950, p. 1.

[4] Editorial, Farm Bureau News, April 6, 1950.

[5] Corps of Engineers: Report of Excess Real Property, Fort Casey, April 20, 1954, Manuscript.

[6] GSA Federal Property & Administration Service Act, Quitclaim Deed, December 2, 1955; Washington Parks and Recreation Commission, Fort Casey Property file, Olympia, Washington.

[7] Mickey Clark, private interview held in Coupeville, Washington, May 10, 1986.

[8] Ibid.

[9] Roy Evans, private interview held in Oak Harbor, Washington, June 16, 1985.

[10] John M. Blum, *et al. The National Experience* (New York: Harcourt, Brace and World, Inc., 1968), p. 777.

[11] Roy Evans, private interview.

[12] Evans, interview.

[13] Ibid.

[14] Lewis, *Seacoast Fortifications*, pp. 132-133.

[15] Article, *Whidbey News Times*, November 30, 1961.

[16] Fort Casey Property file: Washington Parks and Recreation officer, Olympia, Washington.

[17] Article, *Whidbey-News Times*, May 9, 1963.

[18] Article, *Whidbey-News Times*, October 21, 1965.

[19] In a small way I too was a part of the support. In 1964 I was a student at Oak Harbor Junior High and can still remember people who came to the school asking for contributions. I can recall how disappointed I was that they came after lunch and not before. I would have gladly given all my lunch money for what I considered a truly noble cause instead of the mere quarter that I had left.

[20] Article, *Whidbey-News Times*, February 29, 1968.

[21] Jim Collins, private interview held in Burlington, Washington, August 7, 1989.

[22] Dick Clifton, private interview held in Olympia, Washington, during June 19, 1986.

[23] Jim Collins, private interview.

[24] Dick Clifton, private interview.

[25] Jim Collins, private interview.

[26] Jim Collins, private interview.

[27] Fort Casey Property file.

[28] Ibid.

[29] Lewis, *Seacoast Fortifications*, p. 133.

SELECTED BIBLIOGRAPHY

Primary Sources (Published)

Blum, John M., et al. *The National Experience:* New York: Harcourt, Brace and World, Inc., 1968.

Cook, Jimmie Jean. *A Particular Friend, Penn's Cove.* Coupeville: Island County Historical Society, 1973.

Earle, Edward Mead., ed. *Makers of Modern Strategy.* Princeton: Princeton University Press, 1952.

"Establishing the Navy Yard, Puget Sound," *Washington Historical Quarterly;* Vol. II (October, 1907), pp. 356-357.

Fairchild, Byron, and Conn, Stetson: *The United States Army in World War II, The Western Hemisphere: The Framework of Hemisphere Defense;* Washington D.C.: Office of the Chief of Military History, 1960.

Fine, Lenore, and Remmington, Jesse A: *The United States Army in World War II, Corps of Engineers: Construction in the United States.* Washington D.C.: Office of the Chief of Military History, 1972.

Gregory, V. J.: *Keepers at the Gate.* Port Townsend: Port Townsend Pub. Co., 1976.

Hogg, Ian. *Coast Defenses of England and Wales: 1856-1956.* London: David & Charles, 1974.

Hogg, Ian: *The History of Fortifications.* New York: St. Martin's Press, Inc., 1981.

Kellogg, George Albert. *A History of Whidbey's Island;* Island County: Island County Historical Society, 1934.

Lewis, Emanuel Raymond. *Seacoast Fortifications of the United States: An IntroductoryHistory.* City of Washington: Smithsonian Institute Press, 1970.

Mahan, A. T. Major: *Operations of the Navies in the War of American Independence.* New York: Greenwood Press, 1913.

Risch, Erna. *Quartermaster Support of the Army: A History of the Corps 1775-1939.* Washington D. C.: U.S. Government Printing Office, 1962.

Russell, Francis: *The Shadow of Blooming Grove.* New York: McGraw Hill, 1968. 212.

U. S. Congress. *House Report No. 86;* (Ser. 1145), 37th Cong., 2nd Sess., 1850.

U. S. Congress. *House. Exec. Doc. No. 49;* (Ser. 2395, 2396), 49th Cong., lst Sess,, 1886.

U. S. Congress. Senate. *Reports on Fortifications upon Puget Sound.* Senate Ex. Doc. No. 165 (Ser. 2513), 50th Cong., lst Sess., 1888.

Weigley, Russel F. *History of the United States Army.* New York: Macmillan Company, 1967.

Weigley, Russell F. *Towards and American Army.* New York: Columbia University Press, 1962.

Newspaper Articles

Seattle Times. "Thieves Cripple Ft. Casey Guns," March 6, 1938. Seattle Times. Untitled article, April 17, 1950, p. 1.

Whidbey-News Times. "Fort Casey Fires Salute," Friday, September 26, 1901.

Whidbey-News Times. "Two Three-inch Cannons Installed at Fort Casey," May 9, 1963.

Whidbey-News Times. "Governor Proclaims 'Guns for Casey' Month," October 21, 1965.

Whidbey-News Times. "Big Guns Ready for Voyage to Whidbey," February 29, 1968.

Primary Sources (Unpublished Works)

Bailey, Joseph M. "The Defenses of Puget Sound," Washington State Library, Olympia, 1966. (typewritten)

Corps of Engineers. *Report of Excess Real Property, Fort Casey, April 20, 1954* (manuscript). Seattle Office GSA.

Corps of Engineer Files, Record Group No. 77, Box 293, File No. 381-420 (1890 to 1898) all dealing with the procurement of the land and initial beginnings of construction. National Archives, Seattle Branch

Corps of Engineer Files, Record Group No. 77, miscellaneous files boxes 249-266, (1896 to 1903) dealing with construction. National Archives, Seattle Branch.

Corps of Engineers Files, Record Group No. 77, miscellaneous files boxes 241-248 (1898 to 1906), 249-266 (1896 to 1903), 291-296 (1890 to 1898) all dealing with construction at Fort Casey. National Archives, Seattle Branch.

Corps of Engineers Files, Record Group No. 77, miscellaneous files boxes 298-307 (1905 to 1930) covering daily and monthly reports of activity at Fort Casey. National Archives, Seattle Branch.

Corps of Engineers Files, Record Group No. 77, miscellaneous files boxes 298-307 (1905 to 1930), 314-325 (1905 to 1930) covering defensive preparations and preparedness. National Archives, Seattle Branch.

Corps of Engineers Files, Record Group No. 77, miscellaneous files boxes 308-313 (1930 to 1945), 326-332 (1930 to 1945) covering the Modernization

Program before and during World War II. National Archives, Suitland, Maryland Branch.

Hussey, John A. "A Short History of Fort Casey, Washington," National Parks Service, 1956. (type written manuscript.)

Interviews

Bates, Mel. Private interview held in Anacortes, Washington, April 13, 1985.

Clark, Mickey. Private interview held in Coupeville, Washington, April 2, 1985.

Clifton, Dick. Private interview held in Olympia, Washington, June 19, 1986.

Collins, Jim. Private interview held in Burlington, Washington, August 7, 1989.

Engom, Roy. Private interviews held in Oak Harbor, Washington, November 8, 1970, March 30, 1985, and May 29, 1985.

Franzen, Daryl. Private interview held in Coupeville, Washington, August 2, 1988.

Izban, Richard. Private interview held in Anacortes, Washington, April 5, 1985.

Juvet, Henry. Private interview held in Ferndale, Washington, July 22, 1988.

Lee, Don. Private interview held in Coupeville, Washington, May 4, 1985.

Smith, Billie. Private interview held in Coupeville, Washington, April 21, 1985.

Sutton, Donald. Private interview held in Anacortes, Washington, April 3, 1985.

Thesenvitz, Frank. Private interview held in Seattle, Washington, November 25, 1970.

VanDemark, Jess. Private interview held in Ferndale, Washington, July 22, 1988.

Secondary Sources (Published)

Arnold, Major H. H. *Post War Development of Aerial Observation of Artillery Fire*, Journal of the United States Artillery, Vol. 55 No. 6, December, 1921, p. 509.

Cowell, Ray Theodore. "History of Fort Townsend," *Washington Historical Quarterly*, XVI (October, 1925), pp. 284-285.

Gough, Barry M.. *The Royal Navy and the Northwest Coast of North America, 1810-1914.* Vancouver: University of British Columbia Press, 1971.

Green, Constance McLaughlin.; Thomson, Harry.; and Root, Peter C. *The Ordnance Department: Planning Munitions for War.* Washington D. C.: U.S. Government Printing Office, 1955.

Heiston, James A. *The Sinews of War: Army Logistics.* Washington D.C.: U.S. Government Printing Office, 1965.

Hughes, H. Stuart. *Contemporary Europe: A History*, New Jersey: Prentice-Hall., Englewood Cliffs, 1976.

Kirkpatrick, Major Charles Edward. *Archie in the A.E.F.: The Creation of the Antiaircraft Service of the United*

States Army, 1917-1918. U.S. Army Air Defense Artillery School, 1984.

McCurdy, James G. *By Juan de Fuca's Strait*. Portland: Oregon, 1937.

Murray, Keith A. *The Pig War*. Tacoma: Washington State Historical Society, 1968.

Peterson, Harold L. *Forts in America*. New York: Charles Scriber's Son's, 1964.

Richardson, James D., ed. *A Complication of the Messages and Papers of the Presidents*. 10 vols. Washington: Government Printing Office, 1907.

Squire, Watson C., "Military Posts on Puget Sound," Speech in the Senate of the United States, Washington, February 28, 1895.

Shrader, Grahame F. *The Phantom War in the Northwest*. Washington: GPD, 1969.

U. S. Congress. House. *Report of Chief of Engineers*. House Doc. No. 2, Part I(Ser, 3631), 55th Cong., 2nd Sess., 1898.

United States War Department., *Military Reservations*. Washington, 1942.

Secondary Sources (Unpublished)

Corps of Engineers, Plans and specifications for Admiralty Head, Wash., Light Station. 13th L. H. District, Portland, Oregon, July 5, 1901. (12 sheets in custody of Seattle Office, GSA).

Murray, Keith. Private interview held in Bellingham, Washington, August 11, 1986.

INDEX

149th C. A. C., 57
14th Coast Artillery Regiment, 88, 90, 101, 118
248th Wash. National Guard, 101
2nd Balloon Company, 82, 85
56th Amphibious Tank & Tractor, 123
63rd C. A. C., 50
71st C. A. C., 50, 57
85th C. A. C., 57

A. E. F., 81
Admiralty Head, 8, 23, 25, 26, 28, 32, 35, 94, 122
Admiralty Head Lighthouse, 29, 39, 41
Admiralty Inlet, 8, 10, 14, 15, 42, 59
Alaska Gold rush, 28
Ammunition, 21
AMTB defense, 100
Antiaircraft batteries, 62, 79, 84, 95, 100, 107, 108, 111, 112, 113, 122

Balloon Hanger, 82, 83, 85, 95
Bates, Mel, 109, 110, 116, 117, 118
Belgian cement, 31
Bonneville, Benjamin, 10, 28
Breech-loading, 20, 21
Bremerton Navy yard, 8, 26
Brialmont, Henri, 18
Buffington-Crozier, 46, 49

Casey, Thomas Lincoln, 35
Charleston harbor, 9
Chicago Beach, 60
Civil Defense, 128, 141
Civil War, 15, 16, 17, 18
Clark, Mickey, 88, 131
Cleveland, Grover, President, 10
Coast Artillery, 50, 57, 115, 123
Coastal Defense, 8, 9, 20, 78, 85, 95, 142
Coe, Frank W., 86
Collins, Jim, 137, 138

Corps. of Engineers, 13, 28, 31, 36, 53, 91, 125
Craig, Malin, 94, 98
Crockett's Lake, 32, 58, 60
Cunningham, James H., 99, 110

Disappearing carriages, 26, 46, 49
Disappearing rifles, 29, 30
Dollar, John, 60
Donation Land Law, 12, 28
Douglas, Sir James, 13
Duane, J. C., 26

Eastwich, Philip, 31, 32
Ednicott, William C., 24, 26
Elliott, George, 15
Endicott Board, 24, 25, 26, 46
Engom, Roy, 101, 104, 106, 107, 112, 113, 114, 118
Esquimalt, 13, 15, 23
Evans, Daniel J., Governor, 133, 139
Evans, Roy, 128, 129

Flat-trajectory weapons, 24, 46
Fort Flagler, 8, 35, 61, 62, 90, 94, 99, 119, 125
Fort Morgan, 17
Fort Pulaski, 17
Fort Wagner, 17
Fort Ward, 58, 90, 94, 99, 119
Fort Whitman, 58, 90, 94, 99, 119
Fort Worden, 8, 10, 61, 82, 90, 98, 101, 123, 125
Fortifications Board, 26
Franzen, Daryl, 123

General Wilson, launch, 61
GSA (General Services Admin.), 125

Halleck, Henry H., 9
Harbors of refuge, 11, 14, 25
Harding, Warren G., President, 86
Harney, William, 13

Henderson, transport, 86

Isolationists, 99
Izban, Richard, 103, 104, 107, 110, 116, 118

Jedele, Emerson, 103, 104, 112, 113, 117, 118
Juvet, Henry, 70, 73, 74, 76

Kellogg, John, Dr., 26, 28, 43

La Glorie, 18
Lee, Don, 99, 104, 106, 115, 116, 118
Lighter-than-air craft, 81, 82

Mahan, Alfred Thayer, 22, 54, 57
Maine, Battleship, 32
Maney, Goerig, & Rydstrom, 31, 32
Marrowstone Point, 8, 15, 23, 26, 28, 35
Marshall, George C., 99
Miles, Nelson A., 22, 23, 24
Modernization Program, 99, 100, 110
mortars, 24, 49

National Defense Act, 66, 94, 98
National Guard, 62, 69
Nelson, William, 90, 99, 122

Pearl Harbor, 104
Point Wilson, 8, 10, 15, 23, 25, 26, 28
Polk Commission, 11
Puget Sound, 8, 10, 12, 14, 25, 26, 43
Putnam, Alfed, 35, 36

Quartermaster Corps, 39, 85, 91

rapid-fire guns, 24, 49
Report of 1860, 13, 14, 15
rifled artillery, 16
Roosevelt, Franklin, President, 94, 99, 104
Roosevelt, Theodore, President, 54, 57

San Juan Islands, 12, 13, 24
Seattle Pacific College, 126
Selective Service Act, 101
Sherman, Wilbur, 133
Smith, Billie, 91, 109
Smith, Persifor F., 11
Spanish American War, 32, 49
Stoneman, George, 11
Stott, Gerald R., 135
Striped Peak Battery, 122
Sub-caliber, 61, 70
Supplimentary Appropriations Act, 98
Sutton, Donald, 116, 118
Switchboard, 81, 84, 87

Taft Board, 50
Thesenvitz, Frank, 69, 73, 76
Third system forts, 17, 19, 20
Totten, Joseph, 13, 14, 22, 23
trolley/tram, 32, 34, 35, 36, 37

Van Dyke, John, 129, 131
Vancouver, George, 10
VanDemark, Jess, 69, 76
Vanderzicht, John, 126, 129

War Mobilization Plan, 94
Washington National Guard, 81, 86
Washington State Parks. Dept., 126, 129, 139
Washington State university, 141
Weapon removal, 78, 79, 81
Whidbey Island, 10, 28
Whiting, W. H. C., 11
Wilson, Woodrow, President, 66
Winslow, E Eveleth, 62
Wint, Fort, 129, 130, 135, 139
World War I, 62, 66, 73
Wright, Luke, 66

Zeilen, destroyer, 86, 87

ABOUT THE AUTHOR

Terry Buchanan, author of Fort Casey, has been fascinated by the retired military post since his first visit on a Sunday afternoon in 1962 as a 14 year old. His interest led him to seek every bit of local information he could find in his home town of Oak Harbor, Washington, as well as talking to men who had been stationed at the fort. Throughout his school years in Oak Harbor he continued to visit the fort, talk with local residents about their associations with the fort.

Once he entered college he pursued a teaching degree in History at Western Washington University and wrote his first history of the fort. This eventually led to a Master's Degree with his thesis on "Fort Casey and Coastal Defense". This entailed numerous interviews with surviving soldiers from both the First and Second World Wars and eventually a cross country trip to Washington D.C. to spend a week at the National Archives in Suitland, Maryland. Throughout these years he continued to collect interviews, photographs and all manner of information on the fort and its history.

Terry retired in 2006 after a 34 year career as an elementary school teacher in Anacortes, Washington, but always managed to spend at least one day a year on a field trip with students at Fort Casey. Now living in Sequim, Washington, he finally put all his information and collected photographic record into a printed history of the fort. He has been giving slide presentations of the fort for years and still gives walking tours of the gun emplacements.